Sacramental Letters

SACRAMENTAL LETTERS

Themes in Catholic Literature

Nina Butorac

WIPF & STOCK · Eugene, Oregon

SACRAMENTAL LETTERS
Themes in Catholic Literature

Wipf & Stock
An Imprint of Wipf and Stock Publishers
199 W. 8th Ave., Suite 3
Eugene, OR 97401

www.wipfandstock.com

PAPERBACK ISBN: 978-1-5326-5296-7
HARDCOVER ISBN: 978-1-5326-5297-4
EBOOK ISBN: 978-1-5326-5298-1

I wish to gratefully acknowledge the publishers who have granted permission to use the material quoted in this work: New Directions, for verses from "Hagia Sophia," Harper Collins, for quoted portions of *Pilgrim at Tinker Creek*, and Penguin Books, for excerpts from *Conjectures of a Guilty Bystander* and from *Days of Obligation: An Argument with My Mexican Father*.

Manufactured in the U.S.A.

For my sister, Teri, who taught me to read.
1954–2016

Reading List

Essential:

Albert Camus—*The Fall*

Flannery O'Connor—*Wise Blood*

Everything that Rises Must Converge:
"Revelation" and "Parker's Back"

Thomas Merton—*Emblems of a Season of Fury:*
"Hagia Sophia"

Graham Greene—*The Power and the Glory*

Annie Dillard—*Holy the Firm*

Richard Rodriguez—*Days of Obligation: An Argument
with My Mexican Father:* "Late Victorians"

Recommended:

Annie Dillard—*Pilgrim at Tinker Creek*

Franz Kafka—"In The Penal Colony"

Thomas Merton—*No Man is an Island*

Flannery O'Connor—*Mystery and Manners*

Contents

Preface

WE ARE SUMMONED TO be *in* the world, but not *of* the world.[1] This vocational calling is just odd enough to elicit a Christian response that is often conflicted and confused. There are those who would flee the clamor of the city, finding escape and solace in the woods, in a monastery, or walled somewhere behind hard doors. Others feel called to a spiritual perfection that requires transcendence beyond earthly things. Still others, sadly, prefer to circle the wagons around their like-minded tribe and glare with menace at a world they can only see as a danger and on the attack.

Each response can be, I suppose, a failing at understanding what Jesus meant when he claimed us for God. While it is fitting to say that the Christian disciple does not belong to the world, we must not ignore that other affirmation: *we are in it.* The world is where we find ourselves from the moment we reach awareness. We were created here, in this body and circumstance, and with utter divine intent. Early on we learn that we exist in a place, at a time, and among others who are moving us in a direction we did not ourselves intend. This world, with all of its worldly concerns, is a territory replete with sin and the glory of God. We can reject the sin but not the world. The world is where we rejoice in God's glory.

Sacramental Letters aims (in a small way) to capture that glory; to nudge the reader's vision in a direction that uncovers this hidden mystery of grace, and launches them into a new way

1. John 17:11-19

of seeing. Readers will explore the sacramental themes found in the works of Albert Camus, Flannery O'Connor, Thomas Merton, Gerard Manley Hopkins, Annie Dillard, and Richard Rodriguez—themes of sin, guilt, redemption, grace, suffering, and sanctity—as they are revealed through the sacraments of the church and in the creative craft of each author. In this way, I hope to shine a new light on the writings of these modern authors, as well as challenge the Christian disciple to engage the world with compassion; responding to the longing each one of us has to love the world as Christ loves us.

Acknowledgements

I AM GRATEFUL TO all those who helped form me in heart and mind: To my teachers, who instilled in me a love of literature and thought, and to those friends who have sustained me in my work. I wish to especially thank Dr. James Felak, who carefully read and critiqued this manuscript, and gave considerable time to this project. I am also grateful to Larry Carmignani, Jack Whelan, and Michael Lunde, for their critical reviews, encouragement, and support; and to Gela Gibbons and Fr. Daniel Syverstad, OP, for their unfailing friendship. Finally, I wish to express my indebtedness to the authors of the works undertaken in this study. I value their insight as dearly as I value friendship and can only hope that I am worthy to pass their wisdom along.

Author's Note

THIS BOOK CAME ABOUT from a series of classes that I have taught on the Sacramental Imagination at the parish level. Because each chapter addresses a particular literary work and theme, it is important that the reader be familiar with the main works studied here, ideally reading them along with each chapter. A recommended reading list is provided. For those unfamiliar with these literary works, I trust that this study will inspire you to seek them out.

It is my hope that *Sacramental Letters* will encourage teachers to structure their own Sacramental Imagination course for their high school or college aged students; or that readers will assemble and lead a faith formation course or parish book club within their own faith communities. The thoughts presented in these chapters—when taken one chapter per week—should allow for some lively and enlightening class discussions. A list of review questions is provided in the back of the book as a guide.

Go at it with a broadax! The believing and unbelieving world hungers to learn "the terrible speed of mercy."[1]

1. Flannery O'Connor, *Collected Works*, 478.

1. The Sacramental Imagination

(Flannery O'Connor and those other guys)

I FIRST CAME ACROSS the expression "Sacramental Imagination" in Andrew Greeley's book, *The Catholic Myth: The Behavior and Beliefs of American Catholics.* In the third chapter of his book, Greeley poses this question to his readers: "Do Catholics Imagine Differently?" He then proceeds to explain that, yes, indeed they do. "Religion . . . is imagination before it's anything else. The Catholic imagination is different from the Protestant imagination. You know that: Flannery O'Connor is not John Updike."[1] This piqued my interest. How is the Catholic imagination different, and why might this be so? Greeley explains it this way:

> The central symbol (of religion) is God. One's "picture" of God is in fact a metaphorical narrative of God's relationship with the world and the self as part of the world. . . . The Catholic "classics" assume a God who is present in the world, disclosing Himself in and through creation. The world and all its events, objects, and people tend to be somewhat like God. The Protestant classics, on the other hand, assume a God who is radically absent from the world, and who discloses (Himself) only on rare occasions (especially in Jesus Christ and Him crucified).

1. Greeley, *The Catholic Myth,* 34.

The world and all its events, objects, and people tend to be radically different from God.[2]

"(T)he Catholic imagination," writes Fr. Greeley, "is 'analogical' and the Protestant imagination is 'dialectical.'"[3] This Protestant dialectic leaves God in His heaven and humanity—which is inherently corrupt—in a struggle to transcend the evils of the world. The reformed Christian's task is a spiritual conquest, guided by Holy Scripture and a personal relationship with Jesus Christ, to attain heaven by faith alone. Not all will be saved, only the faithful, only the elect, and we have some idea who those saved individuals are by the example they set in their piety and in their lives. Painting with a very broad brush, one can say that the Protestant imagination tells the story of individuals who, through faith, hard work, discipline, and devotion, overcome adversity and attain the goodness of heaven. There is no need for a mediator between the believer and Jesus Christ; images, saints, priests, and purgatory are not necessary to salvation. It is personal. It is I and God. It is heaven or hell. It is dialectic.

Of course, Protestant sects do differ considerably, one from the other, and so it is always dangerous to engage in broad generalities. One aspect of the Protestant imagination might illuminate Lutheran theology, for example, more than it would Calvinist or Southern Baptist thought. Still, our purpose is to show that there is this general Protestant standpoint, dominant in American culture, which is fundamentally different from the sacramental perspective one finds in Catholic culture. In literature, the Protestant imagination gives rise to the American traditions of Transcendentalism and Individualism, as exemplified in the works of Emerson, Thoreau, and Whitman; then later in Twain's *Huckleberry Finn*, Hemmingway's *The Old Man and the Sea*, and Chopin's *The Awakening*. It is so embedded in our experience that to distinguish it from American culture (in order to name it) is like distinguishing

2. Ibid., 45.

3. Greeley's own introduction to this concept came from the work of David Tracy, whose ideas are further set forth in his "The Analogical Imagination, Christian Theology and the Culture of Pluralism." Crossroad, 1981.

oxygen from the air we breathe. What is the scent of the wind? It is difficult to say. But when the wind carries the fragrance of a rose, or even a corpse, we can know it and then claim a distinction. As for our Catholic concern, what does Greeley mean by an "analogical" imagination? He is stating that our Catholic mind-set inclines toward analogy, where one reality underlies and informs another reality. It would certainly seem so. From our earliest days, Catholics recall churches filled with incense and candles, statues and flowers, bells, ashes, oils, and fonts of holy water. These things are called "sacramentals," each standing alone as natural objects in the world, yet each signifying a deeper mystery of faith. The sacraments themselves (with the exception of the Eucharist, which is the Sacrament of sacraments)[4] are analogical. The Catechism of the Catholic Church states: "The visible rites by which the sacraments are celebrated signify and make present the grace proper to each sacrament."[5]

This notion, then, that the Catholic imagination is different from the Protestant imagination presents a real challenge to the student of literature. What should we make of Catholic literature, and where would we even find it? One could argue that literature is not the natural domain of the Catholic imagination. The natural domain of the Catholic imagination lies in the more sensual arts. In a rather eye-popping essay published by the *New Art Examiner*, art critic Eleanor Heartney makes just this claim. In her essay, Heartney examines the legacy of the Catholic Church and the influence it has had on contemporary art. Presuming that her secular audience might be hostile to this assertion, she supports her view with a brief "delve into theology" and explains:

> Catholic doctrine holds that the human body is the instrument through which the miracle of man's salvation from sin is accomplished. As a result, all the major mysteries of the Catholic faith—among them Christ's Incarnation, his Crucifixion and Resurrection, the Resurrection of the faithful at the end of time, and the

4. *Catechism of the Catholic Church*, 1211.
5. Ibid., 1131.

Transubstantiation of bread and wine into Christ's body
and blood during the Mass—center around the human
body. Without Christ's assumption of human form, there
could be no real sacrifice, and hence, no real salvation
for mankind. . . .
All of this is of course in stark contrast to the Protestant emphasis on biblical revelation as the primary
source of God's truth. . . . Sensual imagery and sensual
language are seen as impediments, rather than aids to
belief. The body and its experiences are things to be
transcended. . . . The tension between Catholic and Protestant sensibilities outlined here can be summed up as a
conflict between the Catholic culture of the image and
the Protestant culture of the word. Catholicism values
sensual experience and visual images as essential tools
for bringing the faithful to God. By contrast, American
Protestants depend for their salvation almost exclusively
on God's Word as revealed through the Holy Bible. . . . [6]

It is no coincidence that the invention of the printing press
and the first stirrings of the Protestant Reformation occurred at
the same moment in history. With the aid of the printing press
reformers were able not only to foster their ideas to the Christian
world but to print and distribute the Bible in the vernacular of the
people, something the Catholic Church rigorously opposed. In a
very important way, the Bible and the written word became the
domain of the Protestant imagination. In Protestant culture, this
has translated into a rich literary tradition.

But what of the fiction writer who is Catholic? Where are our
Catholic authors? How does the "sensual imagination" translate
into the written word for us?

In the early part of the twentieth century, Catholic periodicals were asking these same questions, especially with regard to
American literature. While there were some excellent European
classics, and a wonderful body of Russian literature grounded in
the sacramental, American Catholicism had still not produced a

6. Heartney, "Blood, Sex, and Blasphemy: The Catholic Imagination in
Contemporary Art," 2-3, 7.

coherent, literary legacy. By mid-century, with few exceptions, this was still the case.

In a 1952 essay entitled "Catholic Orientation in French Literature," Wallace Fowlie wrote:

> American literature is quite thoroughly non-Catholic. There has never been in this country anything that would resemble a Catholic school of letters or movement in literature. It is true that in 1949 a Catholic magazine was founded, *Renascence*, concerned with art and literature, but the title was ill chosen. It is difficult to have a renascence of something that never existed.[7]

As for European literature, this sensual imaging is more profoundly embodied in poetry. Dante Alighieri, the famed Italian poet of the *Divine Comedy* and our great precursor, is the first to come to mind as a master of powerful, visual verse; as is Petrarch, his contemporary and countryman who ushered in the first stirrings of humanistic thought. And while the Renaissance which followed and flowered in southern Europe owes a considerable debt to the writings of these great Italians, it was largely a renaissance of the tangible arts, and less of literature.

Centuries later the French Symbolist poets of the nineteenth century, most especially Baudelaire and Claudel, began to develop the idea that religious symbolism and poetic symbolism are very much the same. Claudel speaks of nature as a temple, each part of which possesses a symbolic meaning. How is this different from St. Thomas Aquinas, who called the universe a general sacrament which speaks to us of God? Indeed, the writings of St. Thomas had a profound and lasting influence on the French literary world. The renaissance of medieval philosophy, that school of thought known as Neo-Thomism, began its movement in France. St. Thomas provides the French poet with a sacramental aesthetic, "according to which the universe is the mirror of God."[8] It is important to note that this seed of Thomistic thought does not die on the continental shores, though it barely managed to reach beyond the usual

7. Fowlie, "Catholic Orientation in Contemporary French Literature," 225.
8. Ibid., 237.

Catholic circles. That is until a young woman who raised chickens in Georgia started writing stories in the 1950s.

Flannery O'Connor, self-schooled in Thomistic thought, managed to contribute two novels and a number of short stories to American letters before her life was cut short at the age of thirty-nine. And yet she really does stand out as one of America's great prose writers, one whose sensibilities and personal faith were profoundly Catholic, and whose stories are steeped in the sacramental. O'Connor regarded her talent as a gift, but it was not an unconscious gift. She knew what she was about. Echoing St. Thomas, who said that the artist is concerned with the good that is *made*, she asserts that "fiction is so very much an incarnational art."[9] Words made flesh.

In an essay on the "Novelist and Believer," O'Connor tells us:

> St. Augustine wrote that the things of the world pour forth from God in a double way: intellectually into the minds of the angels and physically into the world of things. . . . [The aim of the artist is] to render the highest possible justice to the visible universe. . . . The artist penetrates the concrete world in order to find at its depths the image of its source, the image of ultimate reality.[10]

This view is at the heart of the sacramental imagination.

The central mystery of the Catholic faith is the Incarnation, that mystery through which God became man and dwelt among us. And the great lesson of the Incarnation has become the pivotal theme of contemporary Catholic literature. In his essay on French Literature, Wallace Fowlie concludes with this remark:

> One wonders if Claudel . . . is the only one close to the Dominican [Thomistic] interpretation: Grace does not destroy nature, but perfects and raises it. Despair is not the ultimate secret. Claudel believes in a theocentric humanism. Nothing is more exultant than this conception

---

9. Fitzgerald, *Flannery O'Connor, Mystery and Manners*, 68.

10. Ibid., 157.

of the universe. When the Word became Flesh, it assumed the universe.[11]

My guess is, in 1952, Mr. Fowlie had not yet stumbled upon the hen-house Thomist in Georgia.

While this might seem very well and good, even perhaps a bit heavy-headed, it takes more than great writers to form a great literary tradition. It takes intelligent readers as well. In this vein, Flannery O'Connor presents us with a more personal and immediate challenge.

In a speech delivered to an audience of would-be Catholic novelists, she tells them that "one of the most disheartening circumstances that the Catholic novelist has to contend with is that he has no large audience he can count on to understand his work."[12] For O'Connor, the modern secular world, which makes up most of the Catholic writer's audience, does not believe in the theological truths of the Catholic faith, which is the foundation of the writer's universe and imagination.

> It does not believe in sin, or in the value that suffering can have, or in eternal responsibility, and since we live in a world that since the sixteenth century has been increasingly dominated by secular thought, the Catholic writer often finds himself writing in and for a world that is unprepared and unwilling to see the meaning of life as he sees it.[13]

Of course, the unbelieving world does not make up the author's entire audience. And while it may be fair to say that Protestant believers are likewise confused by the Catholic imagination, one expects there would be a few Catholic readers who share the theological truths of the faith. It is hoped that these would be able to grasp the analogical underpinnings of the sacramental. However, O'Connor suggests that this is rarely the case. In a letter to

---

11. Fowlie, "Catholic Orientation in Contemporary French Literature," 241.

12. Fitzgerald, *Flannery O'Connor, Mystery and Manners*, 181.

13. Ibid., 185.

a friend she writes: "the average Catholic reader was a Militant Moron."[14]

Not exactly flattering.

I would like to think quite a lot has changed since 1956, when she first penned those words, but this seems unlikely. The world has certainly become more secular, and even less equipped to understand the themes that underlie the Catholic mind-set. As for the average Catholic reader, well, our situation is not hopeless. It is possible that we have lost much of our sacramental temperament to the secularized world view, or to a more abstract, transcendent expression so common in American Protestant literature. It is also possible that some of our Catholic sensibilities remain, lingering, so to speak, in the vaulted arches of our memory. Fr. Greeley would surely have agreed with this assessment. He would say that it is there, it has always been there, and it needs only to be recognized, and nurtured, and named.

14. Fitzgerald, *Flannery O'Connor, The Habit of Being*, 179.

2. Stories and Sacraments

Stories

ASK ANY GATHERING OF attentive adults—or even children—to recall their earliest memory,[1] and more often than not they will recollect an image of some *thing* (a toy, a blanket, a clock on the wall), usually centered within a particular event. For example, they may describe their mother's face, smiling, in a room full of light, or a toppled tree they saw in the yard after a storm. Our first memories emerge as we move from infant self-absorption to wonder at the things outside ourselves. Through our senses and by our very nature we are directed outward to engage the world. When we continue the experiment to draw out new memories, we find that we are inclined to embellish the recollection; our minds fill in the blanks with later context, feelings, and names. Where were we? Who else was there? What was the action or event that managed to etch itself into our budding brains? How did it affect us? To begin this back-action process of recollection is to begin to tell a story; and story-telling is something we have been doing since the days of caves.

But what is a story? In its simplest form, a story tells of an event, peopled with characters and ordered by plot. This plot is usually structured upon an arch; where the beginning sets the place and time, introduces the characters, and often alludes to some conflict ahead; the middle provides the action surrounding

1. Appendix 1.

the main event, putting the characters into the heart of the conflict; at the end, the conflict is resolved and the story moves the characters, now changed, forward into a new reality. This is the standard formula for most stories and folklore. The ancients introduced complications and twists to their stories, such as the tragic hero, the mythic intervention of the gods, or moral lessons to be learned, but essentially, the story remains structured upon this simple arch.

In Andrew Greeley's essay, "Why I'm Still A Catholic," the author emphasizes the primacy of Catholic stories even over doctrine: "The doctrines are latent in the stories," Greeley explains. "Both are necessary, but the stories come first." It stands to reason. The main event (and its revelation) takes place in history, and the witnesses to this event retell the story over time. The event precedes the telling, and the telling precedes the written script. Church doctrine, meant to safeguard the teaching, comes much later. "Doctrine never exhausts the truth and the beauty of story. Thus, if I am asked whether I believe in the Madonna and Child or the Incarnation, my answer is that they are one and I believe in both."[2] The Madonna and Child are the story, the Incarnation is the doctrine, and God becoming man is the event.

As we have seen, in simple form, there is always an event taking place inside a story, one that usually causes some change in the characters. Even in our modern and post-modern literature this event can be found. Even in the chaotic array of anti-heroes, absurdist dead-ends, and meandering stream-of-consciousness narratives, something always happens. If it didn't, there would be nothing to say (or read about). Even Godot is worth waiting for!

Case in point: "Nothing is going to happen in this book," Annie Dillard warns us at the beginning of Holy the Firm.[3] But she is not being entirely truthful. She is skirting a very substantial incident that does indeed happen in the book. She just chooses not to tell us very much about it, preferring to layer image upon image, symbol upon symbol, in order to bring out the sacramental

2. Greeley, "Why I'm Still A Catholic."
3. Dillard, Holy the Firm, 24.

character of the event and its effect on her, the witness and writer. This is exquisite story-telling, and it is, I believe, particularly Catholic. When does a story become a Catholic story, then? Surely sacred Scripture, the parables of Jesus, and the lives of the saints are all "Catholic stories" (though not exclusively, of course). So what is it about *Holy the Firm*, for example—a work written by a lapsed Presbyterian who was intrigued with Catholicism—that makes it particularly Catholic, as I claim?

This is the essential question that I will attempt to answer in this book, about *Holy the Firm* and many other great works that are steeped in the sacramental character of the Catholic faith. The answer to this question will not come easily. It will not be plainly stated. Instead, I would encourage the reader to tap along the skin of this onion in order to reveal, layer by layer—depth on depth—a vision that triggers one marvelous insight into the nature of our art, our stories, and our lives.

In order to begin this exploration, we will need to first take a closer look at the sacraments of the Catholic Church.

Sacraments

St. Augustine defined a sacrament as "a sign that gives grace." Grace in this context is a favor, a pure gift from God, which aids us in becoming holy. A more expansive definition of a sacrament is found in the new *Catechism of the Catholic Church* (revised in 1994):

> The sacraments are efficacious signs of grace, instituted by Christ and entrusted to the church, by which divine life is dispensed to us. The visible rites by which the sacraments are celebrated signify and make present the graces proper to each sacrament. They bear fruit in those who receive them with the required dispositions.[4]

4. *Catechism of the Catholic Church*, 1131.

"Efficacious signs of grace" are God's favors which have their *effect* on the recipient (immediate and lasting) because Christ himself is at work in the sacraments. The sacraments of the Catholic Church were "instituted (established) by Christ" during his earthly ministry, as witnessed for us in the gospels. The human actions of Jesus are divine actions because Jesus is divine. In turn, these divine actions are deeds in visible form, accessible to our human way of experiencing the world, because Jesus is also human. Christ's human actions—his life, death, and resurrection—are an expression in human form of the mystery of divine love. "Divine life" is sanctifying grace; that grace which makes us holy and worthy of heaven. We become by grace what Jesus Christ is by nature: children of God.

There are seven sacraments in the Catholic Church: baptism, reconciliation (penance), holy Eucharist (communion), confirmation, matrimony, holy orders, and the anointing of the sick (last rites). These are, essentially, seven outward signs that point to Christ's infinite, redemptive action. The outward sign is a visible, finite symbol that is used to signify the hidden, infinite grace behind each. For example, in the sacrament of baptism water is used to signify the cleansing of the baptized, washed clean of original sin; but it also makes present the pouring out of God's sanctifying grace upon the newly initiated, sealing them for Christ, and providing them with the many gifts proper to their baptism.

The rites of the sacraments not only signify the grace (they are not *simply* allegory or symbol), *they make the grace present*. The sacraments are not merely gestures or rituals or professions of faith. They make what we believe *more real*. They are, fundamentally, an encounter with Christ, who is God's own sacrament. This encounter is an action, a verb, an *event* in which we participate bodily and with wholehearted assent. Because they are an encounter with the divine Christ, the sacraments claim a relationship between us and God and between one another; a relationship that echoes, however faintly, the divine love of the Holy Trinity.

When T. S. Eliot wrote that poetry makes truth more real, he was evoking the sacramental language of the church: "For poetry

. . . is not the assertion that something is true, but the making that truth more fully real to us; it is the creation of a sensuous embodiment."[5] Though the grace that is the reality of the sacrament is hidden, it is *more real* than the outward sign that signifies it. This sacramental view is a way of seeing (or knowing) that extends into our vision of the whole world, as well as our place in it.

Sacramentality

The sacramental perspective, or "sacramentality," recognizes the divine that underpins all of existence; where "reality (is) imbued with the hidden presence of God," as Pope Paul VI stated in his opening address at the Second Vatican Council.

Wendy M. Wright, in her review of Stephen Schloesser's work on the Catholic Imagination, explains sacramentality this way: "The sacramental insight so fundamental to a Catholic view of reality engages us in 'double-business' . . . We are bound to see the finite world as the bearer of the infinite and we must consider that which is singular as of nearly infinite significance. The finite and the infinite are inseparably bound."[6]

Charles Baudelaire, the French master of symbolist poetry, writes: "All forms of beauty like all other phenomena contain something eternal and something transitory—something absolute and something particular."[7] "(T)he composition of beauty is always and inevitably double. . . . (It) is composed of an eternal, invariable element . . . and a relative, circumstantial element. . . . I defy anyone to discover the least gleam of beauty which does not contain the two elements."[8]

This double composition of beauty is essential to our study. It is the language of symbolic poetry but it is more, because the

---

5. Eliot, "Poetry and Propaganda," 601.

6. Wright, "Jesuit Schloesser Weaves Tapestry of Catholic Imagination," 1.

7. Turnell, *Baudelaire, A Study of his Poetry,* 33. From: *Curiosites esthetiques,* 197.

8. Ibid., 33. From: *L'Art romantique,* 69.

sacramental view is out to discover mystery: seeking not only the eternal, but the divine presence behind every sign. In the literary works ahead, we will discover a consistent theme of "double-business." Watch for it. There will be mirrors and reflections; twins and two-faced Januses; signs adorned with shrunken heads and signs that dot the highways; new popes, new jesuses, and faces ablaze, front and back; sin and God embedded in human flesh; bottom rails on top, two candle wicks, and revelation, too. Sacramentality thrives on paradox, irony, and even contradiction. Its artists whisper in the streets the scandalous report that the God-man, Jesus, is one person with two natures. It is the two-lane road we travel.

> This double-business restores us to a place of awe, wonder and humility. (We) locate the Catholic aesthetic precisely at this precarious yet vital point. (The sacramental imagination views the world) not with a sense of despair or outrage but with a sense of compassionate, tragic irony, a sacramental hope in the midst of all that is fallen and lost.[9]

Intuiting Grace

In medieval times, when people wholly believed that spirits and humors affected the human condition, a sacramental view of reality was perhaps more palatable; and one could argue that modernity has put an end to such imaginings, shelving them along with miracles and legends; but the mystic would never submit to such a judgment, and neither would the poet. Strangely, it seems that modern scientists may need to take their place beside the mystics, as they can no longer track along the surface of Newtonian physics. Given what we have learned of the cosmos, the scientist may need to assume a more awkward, poetic stance.

This poetic attitude is not without precedence. The idea that underlying principles govern observable matter was a concept posited by the pre-Socratics in the sixth century, B.C., and again

9. Wright, "Jesuit Schloesser Weaves Tapestry of Catholic Imagination," 1.

by Plato with his perfect forms. Aristotle and St. Thomas defined reality as conforming to a syllogism of 'what' (essence/matter) and 'is' (esse/being). Scientists of the Enlightenment, with their finely tuned instruments, discovered a cosmic and microcosmic realm never before seen. Moderns were soon able to diagram molecules and the structure of proteins, as well as living genes and DNA. With greater precision they discovered the atoms, just as the pre-Socratics had predicted![10] With the advent of advanced mathematics and speedy computers, scientists have had to submit to a new paradigm, one actuated by the strange, contrary behavior of subatomic particles in a universe where matter = energy, and order underlies chaos. Quantum physicists now tell us that the universe is more like a thought than a thing; more like a word than a world; more like a symphony than a soup.

It would seem that the human imagination is uniquely tuned to the concept of a deeper reality underlying the surface plane, even if that reality is humming energy, an idea, a communion, a spirit.[11]

The sacramental imagination might well be an intuition of unimagined grace.

Something is Wrong

We are directed outward by our nature. We are housed in our bodies and our skulls, but our eyes look out at the world. We are *meant* to engage it; and this world that we engage is, sadly, not quite right. Early in our lives we become aware of the fact that something is wrong.

When I was a child—and I was a sensitive child (of course)—I was well aware of this disharmony. I harbored anxieties of abandonment and lived with the dark fear that my parents weren't really my own. Like many young children, I believed that I must have been adopted, that I belonged to another realm, because my experiences told me that a lot of things in my small world were seriously out of

10. Democritis of Abdera, c. 460-370 B.C.

11. See Toolan, "At Home in the Cosmos: The Poetics of Matter=Energy," 8–14.

whack. Perhaps these fears stem from an infantile selfishness that is challenged by the presence of others; or perhaps they are due to some inner sense of justice and the right order of things—a sensibility that is too often violated. Whatever the reason, the insight that something is wrong in the world is a vital discovery.

Plato built his philosophy of ideas (the realm of perfect forms) upon this intuition. For Plato, it was incongruent that the human mind should be capable of imagining a perfect ideal when no perfect thing existed in the world. We observe and experience particulars, not ideals, and these particulars fall far short of perfection. For example, that there exist in the physical world particular horses is quite evident, but "horseness" is a different matter altogether. The ideal of "horseness" is not experienced through the senses but intuited in the mind, and is therefore the only real knowledge we have. "Horseness," Plato asserts, is an ideal form that must exist perfectly in another reality. A better example might be that of a triangle. We can draw meticulous triangles all day long and never manage to do anything more than produce an imperfect model of a perfect ideal. We can conjure and define a perfect triangle in our minds with little effort, but we will never find or produce it. Since this perfect ideal exists apart from the world we experience, it must exist in a different reality, a reality that we once knew before we were born and have since forgotten.

St. Augustine was deeply influenced by Plato, and this notion that perfection exists as an ideal in another realm (the mind of God) is key to the development of his thoughts on original sin. The doctrine of original sin comes from the biblical story of our fall from grace in the Garden of Eden. On account of this primal stain, we are left to struggle in a broken world that cannot be perfected or denied. We see this brokenness in the streets and in our homes; it catches up with us, and it breaks our hearts. While the doctrine of original sin is a theological notion, it is grounded in the basic observation that not all is right with the world.

In a 2014 article for *Commonweal*, John Garvey writes: "The common insight of the great religious traditions is that something is wrong. Something about ordinary human consciousness doesn't work . . . To know you need help that you cannot somehow conjure up through your own power frees you. You have to turn from yourself to something outside yourself, hoping it will be gracious. You have to accept an interior emptiness. . . . The people who are the most open to grace are those who know how broken they are."[12] And yet there are movements and traditions (sacred and secular) that deny this brokenness. With this denial comes a suppression of our deep-down longing for redemption, and for the grace that may still save us. In response to those who refute the traditional doctrine of original sin G. K. Chesterton, ever the wit, gives us this as a springboard for our study:

> Modern masters of science are much impressed with the need of beginning all inquiry with a fact. The ancient masters of religion were quite equally impressed with that necessity. They began with the fact of sin—a fact as practical as potatoes. Whether or no man could be washed in miraculous waters, there was no doubt at any rate that he wanted washing. But certain religious leaders . . . have begun in our day not to deny the highly disputable water, but to deny the indisputable dirt. Certain new theologians dispute original sin, which is the only part of Christian theology which can really be proved. Some . . . in their almost too fastidious spirituality, admit divine sinlessness, which they cannot see even in their dreams. But they essentially deny human sin, which they can see in the street. The strongest saints and the strongest skeptics alike took positive evil as the starting-point of their argument. If it be true (as it certainly is) that a man can feel exquisite happiness in skinning a cat, then the religious philosopher can only draw one of two deductions. He must either deny the existence of God, as all atheists do; or he must deny the present union between God and man, as all Christians do. The new theologians seem to think it a highly rationalistic solution to deny the cat.[13]

So, we will begin with the fact of sin.

---

12. Garvey, "Something is Wrong: That's the Beginning of Wisdom," 8.

13. Chesterton, *Orthodoxy*, 15.

3. Original Sin and Baptism in Albert Camus' *The Fall*

Church Teaching on Original Sin

ONE OF THE GREATEST revelations in Holy Scripture, told in the book of Genesis, is that human beings were created in the image and likeness of God. The Catholic Church teaches this doctrine most emphatically, asserting that this likeness is the foundation of our human dignity, which is the basis of our morality and our call to social justice.

We are spiritual creatures, created to live in friendship with God, but with limits that are set by our created nature. We are contingent beings, dependent upon God for our very existence. We did not bring ourselves into being, we were brought. We were brought as an act of love, made in the image of God, and gifted with a God-like freedom to choose. Our human nature is bound by the uses we make of this freedom.

The story of Adam and Eve is a symbolic rendering of how human beings lost trust in their Creator, and chose to disobey the limits of their nature (by eating from the tree of knowledge). This disobedience subjected human kind to labor, suffering, and death. Every sin is, in essence, a variation on this original disobedience. Sin is always a choice made in freedom. One cannot be coerced into sin. It is a distortion of the very freedom that God has gifted to us. The result of this first sin, then, is the loss of humanity's original holiness. We became afraid of God whose image we have distorted. The consequence of original sin is the perversion of original justice. The Catechism of the Catholic Church explains it this way:

> The harmony in which (Adam and Eve) had found themselves, thanks to original justice, is now destroyed: the control of the soul's spiritual faculties over the body is shattered; the union of man and woman becomes subject to tensions, their relations henceforth marked by lust and domination. Harmony with creation is broken: visible creation has become alien and hostile to man. Because of man, creation is now subject "to its bondage to decay." Finally, the consequence explicitly foretold for this disobedience will come true: man will "return to the ground," for out of it he was taken. Death makes its entrance into human history.[1]

Our fall from grace ushered death into the world. We were not created for death. We consider death horrific, and rightfully so. Our grief at the death of another is legitimate because we were not meant for it. Most of our sins, our distortions of justice, our greed and violent actions, are the consequence of a deep seated fear of death, made real by original sin. Even restlessness, our longing for a greater good, is the result of our once having walked with God and knowing the good of Eden.

Holy Scripture abounds with stories that are variations on the theme of original sin, beginning with the murder of Abel by his brother Cain, and continuing on throughout the history of the Jewish people. Even after Christ's atonement for our sins on the cross, we still fail in holiness. Holy Scripture and the church continually emphasize the universality of sin in our human history.

These are the teachings, but what of our own experiences? Remember our "first thought" reflection? We discover ourselves existing in a world that is not as it should be. We are directed outward toward that world, only to find that it does not conform

---

1. *Catechism of the Catholic Church*, 400. (Emphasis is in the original text.)

to our most inner sense of justice. Instead of true justice, we are wounded by people and circumstances that roil in a fallen state; fallen from justice, fallen from perfection, and fallen from an original innocence that we have not quite forgotten. Sin is "the only part of Christian theology which can really be proved," Chesterton reminds us with a wry smile. And as we interact with others we also discover, sadly, our own sinful selves.

This last discovery demands a response. We can respond with indifference, with unresolved guilt and rage, or with remorse and restitution. The choices we make in our most sacred freedom will govern our lives, our history, and our fate. This is the context I believe we should take with us as we begin to read Camus' *The Fall*.

Albert Camus

Perhaps the most important work we will study in this undertaking is Albert Camus' *The Fall*. Given the title, it should come as no surprise that the major themes of the work center on our fall from grace, original sin, and the sacrament of baptism. Yet for most, it seems, this does indeed come as a surprise. *The Fall* is often critiqued as a bleak work by an agnostic writer whose focus is on the absurdity of modern life, and on one man's inability to save himself from its inevitable end. But I believe this interpretation is shortsighted. While Camus is certainly an agnostic writer (sometimes labeled an atheist, on par with Jean Paul Sartre, which is wholly inaccurate), he called the lack of a religion "vulgar." It might be more precise to describe Camus as a seeker, one whose spiritual journey ended far too early in an utterly absurd car wreck which claimed his life at the age of forty-seven.

While some modern readers might struggle to see the sacramental themes that inspired *The Fall*, others more devout might just as easily ask, "Why study an agnostic like Camus? He can hardly be described as a Catholic writer!" To them I would respond, boldly, that there is probably no greater Catholic work available to us in the twentieth century than Camus' *The Fall*.

Biographic Notes

Albert Camus was born in Algiers in 1913. He was brought up by his widowed mother in great poverty but in the sacramental richness of the Catholic faith. He was baptized a Catholic and received (I would argue) the sanctifying gifts of his baptism. He practiced his faith as a child and was confirmed as a youth. His high school studies led him to the mystics: St. Theresa of Avila and St. John of the Cross. His college dissertation was on the pre-Socratics and their influence on St. Augustine (who had a tremendous influence on Camus' own writings).

However, Camus left the church as a young man struggling with doubt. He was appalled by the evil he witnessed in a world where children suffer, and where all of Europe was cast into the turmoil of World War II, and cast over by the horrific shadow of the holocaust. He condemned the reluctance of Rome to speak out publically against Hitler—and the obscurity of its voice when it did speak—as unconscionable. Without a loud and clear condemnation of evil, Camus wrote, Christianity risked losing "once and for all, the virtue of revolt and indignation that belonged to it long ago."[2]

Crucial to Camus' thought is the notion of the *absurd*, a condition he recognized as the deep disharmony between our own existence and the world. Something is wrong in the way we exist and in the way we engage the world. For Camus, "the absurd is born of this confrontation between the human need (for meaning) and the unreasonable silence of the world."[3] He wrote: "The absurd is essentially a divorce. . . . The absurd is not in man . . . nor the world, but in their presence together. For the moment, it is the only bond uniting them."[4]

Recall Chesterton's two choices from *Orthodoxy*, quoted earlier. When confronted with the absurdity of evil (that man who experiences great joy in skinning a cat), either we must choose

2. Camus, "The Unbeliever and Christians," 74.

3. Camus, "An Absurd Reasoning," 21.

4. Ibid., 22-23.

21

atheism and deny God, or choose Christianity and profess the disunity between man and God (or deny the cat!). Camus chooses the second option—the disunity—but he makes no Christian profession. Rather, he names this disunity "the absurd," and champions our dignity in our noble yet failed efforts to contend against it. This heroic response to the absurd is best expressed in his essay, "An Absurd Reasoning," written in 1940. According to Camus, there are only three ways one can respond to the absurd: either through suicide, which he believed was cowardly; with religion, which he believed did violence to reason since it replaces real experience with a more pleasing, imagined realm; or with acceptance (the absurd does exist) and rebellion (we will continue to fight against it). This last option he defended as heroic since the conflict itself, though unwinnable, is always noble.

Unfortunately, modern interpretations of Camus tend to leave him in absurdity and mark him for that theatre. But I suspect there is greater depth to his religious sympathies than many modern critics are equipped to recognize. In 1940 Camus was just twenty-seven years old. By the time he wrote *The Fall* (published in 1956), he was clearly honing in on the Christian concept of grace, and on the unmerited, sacramental gifts that come from an unrecognized God.[5]

The Fall

I have to confess (and this seems a good place to do so) that I read *The Fall* every year. It never leaves my nightstand. When I teach this course on the Sacramental Imagination, the first reading assignment I give the students is *The Fall*. I tell them that it is a short book and an easy read; they can finish it in a weekend. If they are fast readers they can tackle it in a day. When they return to class perplexed at what they had just gone through, I tell them to go home and read it again. If they are still perplexed, I encourage

---

5. Camus met with Howard Mumma, a Methodist minister, on a regular basis in his later years, and their conversations about the Christian faith are reiterated in *Albert Camus and the Minister*, by Howard Mumma.

them to read it a third time, only backwards. I doubt they ever do but I'm hoping to make a point. What is the point? The point is this: *The Fall* is a confession, "in a way." It is a memory within a memory, driven by a deeper memory, and told by a thoroughly modern, yet haunted man. And it is recounted to a listener as one might recount any recollection: in fits and starts, out of joint, rambling. If you have ever listened to a friend trying to retell a dream, you might note the similarities. Let it happen! Every sentence is a jewel. Let the sentences and images build up in piles around you, and then sit with them a while.

Now let's delve into the novel, bit by bit and front to back, if you please.

The story opens by setting the scene. Here are two gentlemen amid a few scruffy characters sharing a drink in an Amsterdam bar. This isn't Paris, and we know right off that these are two Parisian men, speaking French in a sailor's saloon (strangely named *Mexico City*). The place is peopled with foreigners who can barely communicate their needs to the Dutch proprietor (who isn't interested in them in the least), along with various thieves, some local ladies and their pimps. But why Amsterdam, one wonders. Well, what is Amsterdam but a city of circular canals, where there is fog and dampness all around and a bridge at every turn? Our protagonist doesn't waste much time in reminding us of Dante and his hell. "Have you noticed that Amsterdam's concentric canals resemble the circles of hell?" (*The Fall*, 14) He is a man in exile; from his home in Paris, and from an Eden (a state of grace) that he still longs to possess. Who is this protagonist? He identifies himself as a Parisian lawyer, and a well-known lawyer, to boot. Indeed, in the first paragraph of the book he offers to plead the case of the other man, and he orders a glass of gin from the monolingual Dutchman, solidifying the two's attorney/client relationship at the onset.

He gives his name as Jean-Baptiste Clemence—John the Baptist, Merciful—but it is not his real name. His real name is never given (and there is a reason for this). He is talkative, preoccupied, forgetful, and thoroughly in love with himself. He is a fine physical specimen, and a seemingly good, generous person. Or at least he used to be. He tells his companion that he used to go out of his way to be generous, serving hard-luck widows and orphans, defending the poor and abused, and he is particularly kind to the blind whom he eagerly escorts across the busy streets of Paris. By all accounts, he is a fine, virile, and successful man. He even tips his hat to the blind once he has delivered them safely to the other side of the street. But for whose benefit does he tip his hat? They can't see him bow to them! He is a bit laughable. But this is the earlier Jean-Baptiste, the pre-reflective Jean-Baptiste, the Jean-Baptiste who has not yet awakened from his self-important slumber.

In the narrative, it is a difficult task to unravel the cause of this awakening. He has suppressed the real source, giving us only glimmers and innuendoes of some tragic night. Rather than confess that sin, he tells us that the whirling music of his self-love came to an end the evening he heard laughter behind him, as if it were flowing downstream, while he paused one night on the Pont de Arts. (*The Fall*, 39) Odd. That is not the terrible event. But it does stir his conscience, or perhaps more accurately, it is a blow to his self-satisfied ego. This laughter is friendly enough, but he suspects that it is laughing *at him*, and hauntingly so. He begins to suspect that " . . . the whole universe then began to laugh at me." (*The Fall*, 80)

The next clue he gives us, as he recovers his memory, is of a time when he was sitting in his car at an intersection and slow to leave when the light changed. A blare of horns behind him startled him, and he quickly drove off. Again, this is hardly a memorable event! But that memory jogs another recollection, and our hero recounts an even earlier episode: a time when he was humiliated in public by a slightly-built motorcyclist who had been holding him up in traffic. In the confusion of the ensuing squabble, Jean-Baptiste is duly clopped on the ear by the motorcyclist and called a "poor dope" by a less-than-sympathetic onlooker. This humiliation in front of a crowd of people crushes him. (*The Fall*, 51) Though it is not a particularly memorable event, the fury that erupts in his heart as a result of this humiliation is. Our hero realizes for the first time that he is capable of tremendous hatred, even violence, and that he is not quite the champion of justice that he thought he was.

> When I was threatened, I became not only a judge in turn but even more: an irascible master who wanted, regardless of all laws, to strike down the offender and get him on his knees. After that, *mon cher compatriote*, it is very hard to continue seriously believing one has a vocation for justice.... (*The Fall*, 56)

This looking backwards, this series of recollected memories within memories, is a process not unlike the examination of conscience that Catholics go through as they prepare for the sacrament of penance; and Jean-Baptiste is a self-described judge-*penitent*.

Eventually, after much stalling, he gets to the real event that burns in his conscience, "the adventure I found at the heart of my memory...." In fact, he says very little about it, and describes the episode in an off-handed way, halfway through the book. It occurred "two or three years before the evening when I thought I heard laughter behind me." Here he tells us of the young woman who leapt to her death from the Pont Royal, and of his own inaction when he heard her cries carried downstream. He gives us nothing more. "What? That woman? Oh, I don't know. Really, I don't know. The next day, and the days following, I didn't read the papers." (*The Fall*, 71)

This sin of omission, this refusal to come to the aid of another, goes against the very nature of human love. Love, Bernard Lonergan tells us, is rooted in our sense of connectedness. "It is as if 'we' were members of one another prior to our distinctions of each from the other." "Just as one spontaneously raises one's arm to ward off a blow against one's head, so with the same spontaneity one reaches out to save another from falling."[6] Willing the good of the other, St. Thomas tells us, is love. (Contrast this with Sartre's: "Hell is other people!")

When next we meet our two Parisians, they are on the island of Marken, which Jean-Baptiste describes as a "negative

---

6. Doran and Dadosky, *Collected Works of Bernard Lonergan: Method in Theology*, 56.

landscape," a region below sea level, one that is literally underwater. "A soggy hell indeed!" he cries. "Everything horizontal, no relief; space is colorless and life dead. Is it not universal obliteration, everlasting nothingness made visible?" (*The Fall*, 72) Here is the featureless and futureless horizon of the agnostic and the atheist, modern man gazing out at the gray void. But do look closely at the language Camus is using in this graphic description. Aren't "universal" and "everlasting" words we would use in connection with grace and divinity? Yet here the words are negated by two equally powerful terms: "obliteration," and "nothingness." What might have been a sacramental sign (everlasting grace made visible) is here distorted. Jean-Baptiste cannot deny the visible sign, he can only deny the invisible grace. "Is it not universal obliteration, everlasting nothingness made visible?" The question Jean-Baptiste poses inverts the very definition of a sacrament. And so it is here, at this apex halfway through the work, that our story takes a crucial yet often missed turn.

Before we continue, it really is necessary to revisit the sacrament of baptism, and draw attention to the fact that images and references to baptism abound throughout *The Fall*. In the protagonist's chosen name, Jean-Baptiste Clemence (*The Fall*, 8); in "the soggy hell" (*The Fall*, 72) of Amsterdam, a city of canals, with waters "steaming like a wet wash" (*The Fall*, 12); in the young woman's cry that is "carried by the river to the waters of the Channel, to travel throughout the world, across the limitless expanse of the ocean . . . to await me on seas and rivers, everywhere, in short, where lies the bitter water of my baptism" (*The Fall*, 108); "We shall never get out of this immense holy-water fount." (*The Fall*, 109); and in the frequent allusions to universal guilt (original sin): "We cannot assert the innocence of anyone, whereas we can state with certainty the guilt of all." (*The Fall*, 110) If *The Fall* is replete with images of baptism, then we should review some of that sacrament's matter, form, and graces.

Baptism is the first sacrament because it is, chronologically, the first sacrament instituted by Christ; because it is a rite of initiation; and because it is primary, necessary for all of the other sacraments. Its effects are to take away the stain of original sin, to initiate the baptized into the Christian faith, and to join them in membership with Christ's mystical body.

Since a sacrament is defined as an outward sign of an inward grace, what are the outward signs of baptism? To begin with, the initiate is given a *name*—a name that is spoken and even announced—and then submerged or splashed with *water* while the minister proclaims "I baptize you in the name of the Father, and the Son, and the Holy Spirit." Again, these words are spoken out loud. The inward grace and gifts that are bestowed upon the newly baptized are *forgiveness of sins* and the gift of the *Holy Spirit*. (Acts 2:38) The sanctifying grace that is given is *sealed* upon the baptized for life, preparing them for a life of holiness. As with all sacraments, the initiate must *fully assent* to being baptized; that is, they must say "yes" to the offered grace within the sacrament. Finally, it is important to understand that we are baptized *into the death of Christ* (Romans 6:3); a grace less easily remarked upon.

How are these themes presented in *The Fall*? We have already seen that Jean-Baptist is a thoroughly modern man; a man among men (and women) who are steeped in the petty vanities of original sin. "If pimps and thieves were invariably sentenced, all decent people would get to thinking they themselves were constantly innocent, *cher monsieur*. And in my opinion . . . that's what must be avoided above all. Otherwise, everything would be just a joke." (*The Fall*, 41)

We have seen how, by his public humiliation, Jean-Baptiste has been reawakened, literally dope-slapped into attentiveness, and how he has regained his memory. He can now recall the incident on the bridge when he managed somehow never to risk his life. He feels the shame of this inaction, and the guilt. "Suppressed dives leave one strangely aching," he tells us early on, (*The Fall*, 15) and ". . . the moment I grasped that there was something to judge in me, I realized that there was in them an irresistible vocation for judgment. Yes, they were there as before, but they were laughing."

(*The Fall*, 78) "That perpetual laugh and the laughers had to teach me to see clearly within me. . . ." (*The Fall*, 84)

Jean-Baptiste's solution to his own guilt and shame is to become a judge-penitent, and to counsel the multitude who come to him in the *Mexico City* bar. He does penance in exile. Where he once loved heights in order to dominate, he now resigns himself to the lowest point in Europe, a city kept drained from the flood waters only by a system of siphons, canals, bridges and dikes. Where he once governed as a "new pope" in the Nazi prison camp—allowing himself to be so elected as a joke that he took quite seriously—he now submits to that medieval torture box, the "little ease," which contorts ones very body in excruciating constrictions as an emblem of complete oppression. As a penitent, he must confess the sins of his life to everyone he meets, "indulging in public confession as often as possible. I accuse myself up and down." (*The Fall*, 139)

But he is not only a penitent, he is also a judge. His solution is to accuse himself, yes, but he must also hold up a mirror to all of his confessor-clients in order to prove that they, too, are guilty and stained.

> When the portrait is finished . . . I show it with great sorrow: 'This, alas, is what I am!' The prosecutor's charge is finished. But at the same time the portrait I hold out to my contemporaries becomes a mirror. . . . Then imperceptibly I pass from the 'I' to the 'we.' When I get to 'This is what we are,' the trick has been played and I can tell them off. (*The Fall*, 140)

If the story ended here, then *The Fall* would be pointedly absurd: modern man craving forgiveness, yet always judging his fellow creatures and forever judged by them; each debauched, lowly, pathetic, guilty. But the story does not end in absurdity, there is more, and there is hope. So let us return to the Island of Marken on the Zuider Zee, where our hero takes his crucial turn.

After Jean-Baptiste remarks upon the negative, horizontal landscape and "universal obliteration," his companion balks a little, for
he suggests that the sky is alive and so not everything is dead.

> The sky is alive? You are right, *cher ami*. It thickens,
> becomes concave, opens up air shafts and closes cloudy
> doors. Those are the doves. Haven't you noticed that the
> sky of Holland is filled with millions of doves, invisible
> because of their altitude, which flap their wings, rise or
> fall in unison, filling the heavenly space with dense mul-
> titudes of grayish feathers carried hither and thither by
> the wind? (*The Fall*, 73)

Doves? Those are some pretty strange birds that never sleep or
nest, but hover out of sight. We should recall the baptism of Jesus
by John the Baptist, when Jesus emerged from the waters of the
Jordan River, and how the heavens opened up. Then the Spirit of
God descended "like a dove," and a voice came from heaven saying:
"This is my beloved Son, with whom I am well pleased."[7] The doves
above Holland make their first appearance after Jean-Baptiste has
made a real confession, speaking of the woman who leapt to her
death from the bridge. For the first time he says out loud his sin of
omission. But that is only the first appearance of the doves. They
descend a second time, near the end of the book, when our hero is
sick in bed. Then the doves come down from their height to cover
all of Amsterdam with a thick layer of purity! They also come *for*
Jean-Baptiste. He tells us so:

> Look, it's snowing! Oh, I must go out! Amsterdam asleep
> in the white night, the dark jade canals under the little
> snow-covered bridges, the empty streets, my muffled
> steps—there will be purity, even if fleeting, before to-
> morrow's mud. See the huge flakes drifting against the
> windowpanes. It must be the doves, surely. They finally
> make up their minds to come down, the little dears; they
> are covering the waters and the roofs with a thick layer of
> feathers; they are fluttering at every window. What an in-
> vasion! Let's hope they are bringing good news. Everyone

7. Matt 3:16–17.

will be saved, eh? and not only the elect. Possessions and hardships will be shared and you, for example, from today on you will sleep every night on the ground for me. The whole shooting match, eh! Come now, admit that you would be flabbergasted if a chariot came down from heaven to carry me off, or if the snow suddenly caught fire. You don't believe it? Nor do I. But still I must go out. (*The Fall*, 145)

The doves bring the "good news" (the gospel) that everyone will be saved (even Jean-Baptiste). That is his hope. Though he says he does not believe it, still he must go out!

Remember that the disposition of the recipient for any sacrament is a crucial element in the validity of the sacrament and the gift of grace. If the recipient is not properly disposed—open, and freely accepting—then the sacrament is not valid. We say "yes" to the outward sign and process, but more importantly, we say "yes" to the inward grace that is offered.

Jean-Baptiste so wants to accept this grace! He has seen what human beings are, and he knows the darker side of his own soul. He knows what evil he is capable of doing in this world. He has confessed his crimes committed in the Nazi prison camp, when he drank the rationed water of his dying comrade, who didn't need it since he would soon die. He also knows what he is incapable of doing in this world; saving the woman who leapt from the bridge. Now grace is offered. The heavens open up. The doves invade, fluttering at *every* window! Why wouldn't he go out to accept the bounty of God's love and forgiveness? It's true that his visitor holds him back and is quite upset by his sick friend's rush for the door. "All right, all right, I'll be quiet; don't get upset! Don't take my emotional outbursts or my ravings too seriously. They are controlled." (*The Fall*, 146) But it is also true, sadly, that Jean-Baptiste allows himself to be thwarted. He returns to the comfort of his bed. It is "too late."

We are, as St. Paul tells us, baptized into the *death* of Christ. Can we accept it? We are called to love one another as much as we love ourselves. Can we do it? We are called to that greatest love, to die out of love for another human being. Jean-Baptiste knows this. That is why, with the descent of the doves, he charges his companion to make restitution and sleep on the ground for him. "The whole shooting match, eh!" But neither one of them can manage it. Jean-Baptiste wants to allow the grace of God to solace all the wounds of his life, but he cannot, will not, does not. *Why not?*

After all, our hero is not like those café atheists, the "little sneaks" who "believe only in sin, never in grace." (*The Fall*, 135) No, grace is fluttering at every window. It is accessible, and Jean-Baptiste believes in grace. Only the last paragraph of the book tells us why he does not go out, and what it is that is keeping him from the sacrament that would save him.

After having played his trick on his companion, of moving from the "I" to the "we" of universal guilt, he demands to know the answer to the question at the heart of their memory and their shared failing:

> Then please tell me what happened to you one night on the quays of the Seine and how you managed never to risk your life. You yourself utter the words that for years have never ceased echoing through my nights and that I shall at last say through your mouth: 'O young woman, throw yourself into the water again so that I may a second time have the chance of saving both of us!' A second time, eh, what a risky suggestion! Just suppose, *cher maître*, that we should be taken literally? We'd have to go through with it. Brr . . . ! The water's so cold! But let's not worry! It's too late now. It will always be too late. Fortunately! (*The Fall*, 147)

Jean-Baptiste refuses the grace of baptism (which would name him, and this is why he is unnamed) out of fear for his life. Camus would know that to die with Christ, when taken literally, requires our dying to ourselves for another; and not just figuratively—as some nice platitude of Christian sentiment—but actually, for that person right there in front of us. We are baptized into the death of Christ *at great risk and peril.* But as to whether or not it is too late to act, only the living can decide.

There is so much more one could say about *The Fall*. Camus' themes on justice and judgment, freedom and oppression, and the universal need for a "new pope," are as heavy in meaning as is his treatise on guilt, sin, and grace. However, those themes may need to be worked out in a later study. For now, know that we are not yet finished with *The Fall*. It will be our anchor-hold for the later works we will examine. Just as baptism is the primary sacrament, needed for all of the other sacraments, so too will *The Fall* be our primary literary work, one which is needed in order to grasp the richer meanings found in the chosen works ahead.

4. Guilt and Penance in Flannery O'Connor's *Wise Blood*

THE CHURCH ORDERS THE sacraments according to the events in our lives; but events overlap, fray, celebrate, and injure, apart from any neat order. Is it any wonder, then, that the unseen grace at work in the sacraments also overlaps and spills into every corner of our lives? Grace is fluid and life is messy. There is an order to the sacraments, but the order is not absolute. Still, baptism is the first sacrament and required for all the rest. Baptism initiates us into the faith. Then penance and the Eucharist usually follow, to lift us from our failings and sustain us on our journey. As we near maturity a second initiation rite of confirmation is offered to prepare us for a wounded world. Then there are the vocational sacraments of love (matrimony and holy orders). The sacrament of the sick (extreme unction, last rites) heals us in body, mind and spirit as we age and, if it is God's will, enter into everlasting life with Him at death.

While the sacraments themselves are the foundation of the sacramental, they are not the only sources of grace. They are, indeed, those signs instituted by Christ to give grace, but grace abounds. It is our spiritual duty to be attentive to the grace-filled moments that God allows in this rich landscape. For some, grace is recognized as a whispered sweetness. For others—the hard of hearing—it sometimes takes a good shout! The next author we will study, Flannery O'Connor, did some mighty fine shouting.

Flannery O'Connor

Biographic Notes

Mary Flannery O'Connor was born in Savannah, Georgia, in 1925, the only child of Edwin and Regina Cline O'Connor. Flannery was a self-described "born Catholic" and attended Catholic schools in Savannah until 1938, when the family moved to Milledgeville, Georgia. Milledgeville was the home of Regina Cline, Flannery's mother, and there they were better able to tend to her father's illness, who had been diagnosed with lupus the year before. He died in 1940, when Flannery was fifteen years old.

O'Connor attended public high school and the Georgia State College for women. She later received her Masters of Fine Arts degree from the State University of Iowa and its esteemed writing program. At this time, when she was just twenty-three years old, she began working on *Wise Blood* as a writers' project. In 1948 some chapters of the work were published and the novel won the Publishers Prize for first novel (in unfinished form), based on the first six chapters.

She attended the Yaddo writers' colony at Saratoga Springs, New York, and restructured the novel while studying there. In 1950 O'Connor was diagnosed with lupus and was very seriously stricken by the disease, coming close to death. She moved back home to the Milledgeville farm, Andalusia, to recover her health, and lived alone with her widowed mother. She enjoyed raising chickens and peacocks, which occasionally strut in and out of her stories—as does her very capable mother!

The completed novel, *Wise Blood*, was published in 1952, when she was just twenty-seven years old. O'Connor was petite in stature (5'3"), shy, sly, and she spoke with a heavy Georgian accent. Her southern mild manners often concealed the depth of her thought and character, as well as her wicked sense of humor.[1]

---

1. In Flannery O'Connor's January 1, 1954, letter to Elizabeth and Robert Lowell she writes: "I didn't mean I was fat when I said I was disgustingly healthy. I'm not fat yet but I don't have any room to grow. I just meant I don't look very intelligent. I was in Nashville a couple of weeks ago . . . and met a

She continued to write short stories which were published in various periodicals and earned her considerable respect as a powerful, though often misunderstood, young writer. She is usually tagged as "Southern Grotesque," a member of that odd tradition that welcomes Edgar Allen Poe, William Faulkner, and Truman Capote, but this was a classification she herself rejected. What she wrote, she claimed, was Christian *realism* filtered, naturally, by her faith and her own way of seeing. But what she saw she examined to the teeth, and then told about it without flinching. She did not apply a grotesque mask upon the characters in her works; rather, she presented them with unabashed clarity. She just happened to have a sharper, more critical eye, a keener vision, or perhaps an unequalled honesty that allowed her to name what she saw, unfettered by fear. "The stories are hard, but they are hard because there is nothing harder or less sentimental than Christian realism. . . . When I see these stories described as horror stories, I am always amused because the reviewer always has hold of the wrong horror."[2]

O'Connor completed two novels and a score of short stories in her lifetime, working three hours a day each morning. The treatment she received for lupus in those days caused deterioration of her bones, especially in her hips, and she was confined to crutches for the last years of her life.

She published her first collection of stories, *A Good Man is Hard to Find*, in 1956. In 1960 she published her second novel, *The Violent Bear it Away*. Her second collection of short stories, *Everything that Rises Must Converge*, was published posthumously, in 1965. Flannery O'Connor was finishing her last story, "Parker's Back," in the hospital when she slipped into a coma from the ravages of lupus and died on August 3, 1964, at the age of thirty-nine.

---

man who looked at me a while and said, 'That was a profound book. You don't look like you wrote it.' I mustered up my squintiest expression and snarled, 'Well, I did,' but at the same time I had to recognize he was right." Fitzgerald, *Flannery O'Connor, The Habit of Being*, 65.

2. Fitzgerald, *Flannery O'Connor, The Habit of Being*, 90.

Guilt and Penance

Like *The Fall, Wise Blood* is a tale about original sin. Indeed, when O'Connor completed her first collection of short stories she dedicated the book to her close friends, Sally and Robert Fitzgerald, and wrote to them saying: "Nine stories about original sin, with my compliments."[3] As a devout Catholic, O'Connor was well schooled in the church's teachings on original sin and its consequences, and she used those themes as well-gnawed matter for her stories. And while *Wise Blood* is certainly a story about self-reflection, penance, and redemption (just as *The Fall* is a novel about self-reflection, penance, and redemption), O'Connor moves these themes into deeper waters in ways that Camus could not, or perhaps would not do.

> "*God is not needed to create guilt or to punish.*
> *Our fellow men suffice.*" (*The Fall*, 110)

Too often in our culture guilt is defined as a negative and damaging indictment imposed by other people and destructive to one's healthy self-esteem. While this may be true when authority is misused and when guilt is inflicted as a punishment, it is not the Catholic Church's notion of guilt. According to the church, guilt is one's *own* response to the sin that one has committed. It is the action of one's reflective conscience, centered in the will, and based upon the inherent dignity of the human person. One of the core teachings of the Christian faith is that we are moral beings who have the law of God written on our hearts.[4] To the eyes of faith, then, there is no greater evil than sin, and no greater human need than forgiveness. When we act against our conscience, which is the sanctuary of God, we feel the wounding of guilt in that hallowed place. It is akin to the sting of shame that Jean-Baptiste felt, when he recalled his own grave failings.

3. Ibid., 74.
4. Romans 2:15.

As we have learned, every sin committed is a variation on the original sin of disobedience against God and against our own created nature. Baptism takes away the stain of original sin, but the effects of the sin remain. Our natures, weak and still fallen, will surely allow us to sin again. Because sin wounds God's honor and love, as well as the sinner's own dignity, this wounding requires a response. We ask forgiveness of God and from those we have wronged.

The sacrament that Christ established for the forgiveness of sins is called the sacrament of penance (or confession or reconciliation) which restores the sinner to a state of grace. We must have a conversion of heart to be properly disposed to receive the sacrament of penance; that is, we should be truly sorry for what we have done and no longer harbor the malice that occasioned our sinful act. We should repent in the sense that we should turn back to God and ask for the gift of forgiveness. This asking should be spoken, because we manifest our intentions in words, and expressed to another person who is able to receive it. With absolution, the penitent must perform a penitential act to restore the good and make reparations to the one harmed. The confessor (the priest who hears the confession) will propose an action that the penitent must undertake to restore order, to heal the relationship that was damaged by sin, and to reestablish those good habits that befit a disciple of Christ.

Wise Blood

When we open to the first pages of *Wise Blood*, we are immediately struck by the odd, loveless relationships that haunt Hazel Motes, the protagonist of the story. We find him seated on a train where he is preoccupied with the Negro porter, a man who resembles someone he once knew from his home town. But the porter rebuffs Hazel's assertions, wanting nothing to do with this peculiar white boy who keeps calling him by the wrong name. The grandmotherly Mrs. Hitchcock, seated across from Hazel, makes idle chatter, claiming (in one of her many platitudes) that "life is an inspiration," but she has already sized him up with a glance and rendered her low judgment of him based upon the cheap price tag she sees stapled to the sleeve of his suit. The bird-like women Hazel meets in the dining car, with their bright colored clothing, sharp, blood-red nails, and their cackling taunts, are reminiscent of harpies taking lewd delight in their awkward, young victim. Hazel's childhood home, his memories of an overbearing grandfather, and his time in the army, are all dark recollections of the broken relationships that he has experienced in the past. But for all this, nothing is quite as dark as Taulkinham, the city he aims to make his own.

The reader rightly wonders why this world is so dismal. It seems too bleak to be an honest description of the world we live in. Critics of her work had made these same observations in her lifetime. O'Connor's response is telling:

> What these editorial writers fail to realize is that the writer who emphasizes spiritual values is very likely to take the darkest view of all of what he sees in this country today. For him, the fact that we are the most powerful and wealthiest nation in the world doesn't mean a thing in any positive sense. The sharper the light of faith, the more glaring are apt to be the distortions the writer sees in the life around him.[5]

Hazel Motes is just as distorted as his world. He claims that in Taulkinham he will do things he has never done before. The vagueness of this remark, though hinting at the sexual, is markedly ambiguous. He doesn't know what he is going to do. The message on the men's room wall advertising "the friendliest bed in town" sets him on his hapless course, one that is glaringly counter to any kind of real, loving relationship. But Hazel isn't searching for human love, nor is he attracted to Leora Watts or her friendly bed. "If she had not had him so firmly by the arm, he might have jumped out the window." (*Wise Blood, CW,* 18)

---

5. Fitzgerald, *Flannery O'Connor, Mystery and Manners,* 26; footnote denotation.

These loveless encounters reveal a singular truth about Hazel's world. All is not well in the city. Something is terribly wrong.

> His second night in Taulkinham, Hazel Motes walked along down town close to the store fronts but not looking in them. The black sky was underpinned with long silver streaks that looked like scaffolding and depth on depth behind it were thousands of stars that all seemed to be moving very slowly as if they were about some vast construction work that involved the whole order of the universe and would take all time to complete. No one was paying any attention to the sky. The stores in Taulkinham stayed open on Thursday nights so that people could have an extra opportunity to see what was for sale. (*Wise Blood, CW,* 19)

There are three unique views given in this brief and telling paragraph. The first is Hazel's sightless view, one that is not drawn in by the store fronts or the silver streaked sky. The second is the angle of the people of Taulkinham, who are only looking in at the stores and are paying no attention to the order of the universe. The third view is the omniscient narrative view, which shows us—almost as a grace—the shear and stark reality of what is truly taking place. This juxtaposing of blindness with vision and beauty with kitsch should jar the reader a little. The language is both sublime (the narrative "depth on depth" of sky) and pedestrian (the marketing pitch for that "extra opportunity to see what was for sale.") Language used in this fashion is meant to alert the reader to these remarkable contrasts, directing them to notice the marvelous image of the streaked sky and ponder the construction of the universe for themselves, when they might otherwise have followed Hazel down the street like a stray dog.

"Seeing" is a major theme in *Wise Blood*, just as it was in *The Fall*. In *Wise Blood* we have a fake-blind prophet/preacher, Asa Hawks, as well as the stunning, self-blinding action taken by Hazel Motes. The names of the characters also betray a motif of blindness. Hazel (in a haze) Motes (referring to Jesus' admonishment to those who claim to see: "Thou hypocrite, cast out first the beam out of thy own eye: and then shalt thou see to cast out the mote out of thy brother's eye.")[6] and Asa Hawks, with eyes like a hawk, only pretending to be blind.

This theme of blindness appears again and again in the works we will study. In *The Fall*, we learned how the spiritually blind Jean-Baptiste used to make a show of helping blind people across the street. It is only after his confession that he admits to spitting "daily in the face of all the blind." (*The Fall*, 86) Remember, too, in the Gospel of John, Jesus cures a young blind man and makes it clear to the Pharisees that his blindness is no one's fault. Then, to the accusing Pharisees who presume to know the will of God, Jesus says: "If you were blind, you would have no sin; but now you are saying, 'We see,' so your sin remains."[7] This Scripture passage influences much of *Wise Blood*, especially after Hazel's own immolation. Recall how he subsequently and softly chides Mrs. Flood, his landlady: "If you believed in Jesus, you wouldn't be so good." (*Wise Blood, CW*, 125) Mrs. Flood is delighted by this contorted praise.

When Hazel first comes upon the false preacher, Asa Hawks, he is intrigued by this cruel man, with scars running down each cheek, who claims to have blinded himself for Jesus. Hawks garners pity from other people's crowds and begs for coins while preaching a pay-up-or-die kind of salvation. But Asa Hawks is, in fact, neither blind nor holy. He is just a mean, fake, swindler; out only for money and a soft living. His "bastard" child of suspect purity (Sabbath Lilly Hawks) completes a much distorted picture of familial love. There is no relationship, other than the mutual benefit each gains from the other, and one would just as easily leave the other's company if it profited them to do so. While it is true that Hazel takes a shine to Sabbath Lilly, his own conflicted longings (for Jesus) and his stunted emotions lead him into an awkward courtship that is as comic as it is tragic. But his greater love is hidden, or at least, he is hiding from it.

What is Hazel hiding from? He is hiding from Jesus who lurks behind every tree. Hazel denies Christ, and in so doing he

6. Matt 7:5, *Douay-Rheims Catholic Bible*.

7. John 9:41.

refuses the cross, just as Jean-Baptiste refused it. Indeed, Hazel has a similar insight into original sin, "If I was in sin it was before I ever committed any" (*Wise Blood, CW*, 29), and chooses a life of debauchery as a means to shake loose from any claim that religion might have on him. Like Jean-Baptiste, Hazel needs to make a public renunciation.

The very first thing Hazel does, after securing a woman and a place to be, is start up a new ministry that tells his own version of the truth. It is summed up in his shocking proclamation that "Jesus is a trick on niggers."[8]

On his third morning in Taulkinham, Hazel awakens with the thought "full-grown in his head" that what he must absolutely do now is go out and buy himself a car.

Hazel's encounter with the boy Slade at the used car lot is richly comic, but there is also something important going on with this exchange. We recall that Hazel Motes has decided to begin a new church, the Church Without Christ. He is, as some critics have pointed out, a new St. Paul. And if the reader is not attentive, this boy Slade that Hazel meets at the car lot might easily be overlooked. For three pages, O'Connor gives us a string of unique, sensory details about the child that we should observe closely. We first find the white boy perched and huddled up on top of a gas can. He has a sour expression, a look that is meant "to keep people out." He's wearing a

---

8. It is important, if not crucial, to explain O'Connor's use of the so-called "N" word in her stories. I do this, not as an excuse, but as a clarification of her art. I cannot express more emphatically that Flannery O'Connor is a *realist*. Her task is to see clearly the world around her, to penetrate that reality to its core, and then to present it as honestly as her artistic gifts allow. O'Connor's world was the Deep South from 1925 to 1964. This is the way people spoke, and she used the language of her time and place toward that artistic and sacramental end. But O'Connor does not use such terms in her narrative voice—unless she is in the mind of a character—and her stories do present the evils of racism, as well as the blindness of the well-meaning but often wrong-minded white liberal. Her short story, "Everything that Rises Must Converge," is an excellent case in point. Perhaps she should have seen the dangers of such acute realism, but I doubt it would have changed her prose. The sad legacy of her insistence upon this exactness in her art—proper or not—is that her works are now rarely taught in high schools or colleges, and may well end up in parochial obscurity. That would be a tremendous loss, and a victory for the devil.

raincoat, and a cap pulled low over his eyes, smoking a cigarette that dribbles ashes an inch long. His face is like a "picked eagle's." He is distorted, he snarls, he scrambles between cars like a little beast, and he curses deep in his throat. "'Jesus on the cross,' the boy said. 'Christ nailed.'" But are these really curses?

The image O'Connor paints of the boy Slade should be telling. What is it that sits hunched over and balanced on the high parapet of great churches but the beastly little gargoyle? The name 'gargoyle' is derived from the Latin root word meaning "gargle." Its practical role is to drain rainwater off the rooftop of churches through a gurgling mouth. Its spiritual role is to act as a benevolent sprite and frighten away evil spirits. Listen closely to the boy Slade and you'll discover that these are not curses at all. "All the time he kept saying, 'Sweet Jesus, sweet Jesus, sweet Jesus.'" (*Wise Blood*, *CW*, 41) He is repeating the Lord's name! How revealing that the name "Jesus" (not spoken in vain) should so upset the abusive father Slade, and Hazel as well. The boy isn't cursing, he is *naming*. He knows that Hazel is marked for the Lord. And who were the first to identify Jesus but the demons, as we read in the Gospel of St. Mark: "I know who you are—the Holy One of God!"[9]

This episode depicts Hazel as establishing his new church, the Church Without Christ, complete with gargoyles, recognized by demons, and founded upon the integrity of a $40 car. He bought the car foolishly, blindly, refusing to crawl under it or even raise the hood. As amusing as these pages are, the topic she presents (according to O'Connor) is clearly a matter of life and death. She writes in the 1962 preface to *Wise Blood*: " . . . all comic novels that are any good must be about matters of life and death."[10] Hazel's dysfunctional, dribbling, unsteerable and misaligned "church" shudders down the road with dangerous momentum and questionable brakes! He is set on his perilous mission trusting only in his own flawed judgment, past the "666 posts," and directed as far from Jesus as he can get. The father and the boy Slade, looking exactly alike, stare after him.

9. Mark 1:24.
10. O'Connor, *Wise Blood*, 2.

The Slades are yet another example of a loveless, broken family. There is a real evil (in the Catholic sense of the word) in these disordered relationships. Evil is defined as the absence of good, but more precisely, evil is a negation—a void—where the good *ought* to be. These broken relationships emphasize the sorry state of our fallen world, peopled by flawed, fallen characters in desperate need of grace.

Perhaps no character is as hopelessly flawed as Enoch Emery. The Preacher Hawks is greedy and cruel; Sabbath Lilly, sly, mischievous and lusty; but Enoch is touched with a preternatural astuteness (his wise blood) that confounds Hazel's reasoning. Enoch is the only character who can actually see the dark reality of Taulkinham, where people are unfriendly and where he is consigned to the demeaning task of guarding the city zoo. (Yet he does feel exquisite happiness at belittling the monkeys there!) I suspect this is not because Enoch possesses some kind of instinctual innocence. His wise blood is more on par with stupidity than it is innocence. Yet Enoch does see clearly enough to know that the city is dark and mean and fallen. Like Jonah, he is a reluctant prophet who has been cast out of his own country and forced to live with an old woman who spouts "Jesus all day long." Enoch has no use for this kind of sanctification and flees the old lady's house. When he comes upon Hazel and discovers his Church Without Christ, Enoch is infatuated. He does not want to ever lose sight of him (and Hazel has to hit Enoch over the head with a rock just to escape the lunatic).

Yet Enoch cannot avoid his fate. His wise blood rules him. He is moved, for example, to build a tabernacle in his bedroom but he does not know why. In one telling scene he is driven against his will into a theatre where he must endure three frightful films in something akin to the belly of a whale. This episode in the theatre makes it absolutely clear that Enoch is Jonah, the reluctant prophet:

> I ain't going in no picture show like that," he said, giving it a nervous look. I ain't going in, he said. . . . Two doors flew open and he found himself moving down a long red foyer and then up a darker tunnel and then up a higher

still darker tunnel. In a few minutes he was up in a high part of the maw, feeling around, like Jonah, for a seat. (*Wise Blood, CW,* 78-79)

O'Connor is none too subtle! After the three feature films (*The Eye, The Devil's Island Penitentiary, and Lonnie Comes Home Again*)[11] Enoch makes a dive for the aisle and exits into the street. Once he recovers himself, he sits by the theatre building with a premonition that something is about to occur. It is then that he re-encounters Hazel Motes, who is now preaching about the need for a "new jesus." Enoch is flabbergasted. He knows exactly who this "new jesus" is and where he can find him.

In his preaching, Hazel calls for a savior that does not have blood to waste on redemption. The shriveled mummy that Enoch steals from the museum fits the bill perfectly. Like Jean-Baptiste's call for a "new pope," Hazel's "new jesus" must replace the old one and lead the fallen faithless into a new age. The "new jesus" that Enoch delivers to Sabbath Lilly (now bedded down with Hazel after leaving her despicable daddy) is a vile, bloodless, and repulsive thing, but she does not see it as hideous. Instead, she is captivated. She proclaims him "cute" and holds him like a baby. Here O'Connor paints a diabolical Madonna icon of Sabbath Lilly Hawks with the mummy-christ cradled in her arms. "Call me Mamma now," she says to Hazel. But Hazel reacts with fury. He grabs the mummy and slams it against the wall. "The head popped and the trash inside sprayed out in a little cloud of dust." (*Wise Blood, CW,* 106) He then throws the carcass out the window while Sabbath Lilly shrieks with indignation.

Redemption is the focal point of Christian life. Though Hazel has preached against it by calling for a "new jesus" that has no blood to waste on redemption, when he is confronted with the *very image* of this new deity he is sickened, furious, and has the sudden good sense to destroy the thing. This "new jesus" will never die for love of the world, it will never offer its blood for our salvation. This distorted, shrunken corpse only serves to depict the horror

11. Examine your conscience; repent of your sins; be restored to grace!

of the human condition without Christ. This is what sin does to human beings: complete annihilation, death without hope, mortality without resurrection, "universal obliteration, and everlasting nothingness made visible." (*The Fall*, 72)

Because redemption is a matter of life (with Christ) or death (without), O'Connor paints these startling images to shock the reader into seeing how critical the choice is. She writes:

> The novelist with Christian concerns will find in modern life distortions which are repugnant to him, and his problem will be to make these appear as distortions to an audience which is used to seeing them as natural; and he may well be forced to take ever more violent means to get his vision across to his hostile audience. When you can assume that your audience holds the same beliefs you do, you can relax and use more normal means of talking to it; when you have to assume that it does not, then you have to make your vision apparent by shock—to the hard of hearing you shout, and for the almost blind you draw large and startling figures.[12]

Hazel Motes has established a dangerous church—comically depicted as the high, rat-colored car—but with a deity that is void of divine love and portrayed as a shriveled corpse. This is a false faith. Yet Hazel *is* searching for the truth, and his integrity lies in this search. He denies Jesus because he has convinced himself that Jesus is a lie. But since Jesus Christ is true, as O'Connor would insist, Hazel's search for truth must eventually lead him to Christ who has never abandoned him and who continues to move from tree to tree, from cross to cross, in the back of his mind.

However honest, Hazel's path to truth is corrupted by sin. He is guilty of blasphemy, fornication, pride, and one other very grave offense that sometimes gets overlooked. While preaching his Church Without Christ from the hood of his car, Hazel meets up with his double, and it takes something very much like a mirror to provoke Hazel into committing murder.

---

12. O'Connor, "The Fiction Writer and his Country," 805-6.

Hazel encounters the fake preacher after a conversation he has had with a side-show promoter type, one Onnie Jay Holy (aka, Hoover Shoats).[13] He rebukes Onnie Jay for being a liar and a profiteer. But Shoats, who clearly is a liar and a profiteer, knows a good money-making scheme when he sees one. He hires himself his own Prophet, a consumptive father of six named Solace Layfield, to preach to the drifty after-movie crowds. Layfield imitates Hazel's preaching style while Shoats works the crowd, calling for a 'new jesus' and a new church. This splintered faction of Hazel's own "protestant" remnant infuriates our hero. When Layfield climbs up on the hood of his own battered car and proclaims the "Holy Church of Christ Without Christ," he is mocking Hazel's key doctrine. On top of that he gets it all wrong. What drives Hazel to murderous fury, however, is Layfield's duplicity; he doesn't even believe what he preaches. Hazel is so incensed by this deception that he runs Solace down in the street with his car, and then he backs over him again, just to make sure the deed is done right. Solace, with his dying breath, confesses his sins to Hazel, who bends close to hear.

After the murder, Hazel prepares to skip town. If he is remorseful it is not shown. He spends the night sleeping in his car, thinking about his future and how he will preach the Church Without Christ in some new city.

The next morning, on his way out of town, Hazel is pulled over by a patrolman who asks to see his license. Hazel admits that he does not have a license (no authority to preach) and the officer responds by methodically pushing the rat-colored car, Hazel's church and pulpit, over a cliff: "it landed on its top, with the three wheels that stayed on, spinning." The officer of the state has annihilated Hazel's church. "'Them that don't have a car, don't need a license' the patrolman said, dusting his hands on his pants." (*Wise Blood, CW*, 118)

---

13. A student once pointed out that Onnie Jay Holy was "pig latin" for Jonnie Holy. And as we may know, a shoat is a baby pig.

The destruction of his church humiliates Hazel, though very little is told about this life-changing event. What O'Connor does give us is this:

> Haze stood for a few minutes, looking over at the scene. His face seemed to reflect the entire distance across the clearing and on beyond, the entire distance that extended from his eyes to the blank gray sky that went on, depth after depth, into space. His knees bent under him and he sat down on the edge of the embankment with his feet hanging over. (*Wise Blood*, CW, 118)

We never enter Hazel's head or hear his thoughts, but his fascination with the "blank gray sky," the "distance," the "depth after depth," should remind us, not only of Jean-Baptiste's "negative landscape" on the Zuider Zee, but of the sky that Hazel had ignored on his second night in Taulkinham. This small clue suggests that Hazel has now gained some new insight into the whole order of the universe, which he had missed before.

In the next scene Hazel returns to the boarding house with a package of lime. He informs Mrs. Flood, the landlady, that he intends to blind himself. The violence of this action is not written, but only told from a great distance by Mrs. Flood. It is enough. Now the narrative changes and the story is related from the land-lady's perspective, as we enter her inner thoughts. From this vantage point—one we never were allowed to enter with Hazel Motes—we can gain some insight into her small worries and her empty world, and we may even begin to notice an awakening in her heart.

Penance, as the Catholic Church defines it, is turning away from an attachment to one's self and turning back towards God. Hazel now seems able to recognize his need for penance, to admit his guilt, and to await the forgiveness of God. This is what guilt properly achieves. It turns the sinner around to a different way of seeing and acting and loving. The word "repent" means to "turn around." But this is not the usual understanding of guilt in our culture. As the landlady says to herself: "What possible reason could a sane person have for wanting to not enjoy himself any more?" (*Wise Blood*, CW, 119) The idea of actually doing *penance* is a concept that Mrs. Flood morally opposes. It's foreign. It's popish. It's something a monk would do. "'It's like one of them gory stories, it's something that people have quit doing—like boiling in oil or being a saint or walling up cats,' she said. 'There's no reason for it. People have quit doing it.'" (*Wise Blood, CW,* 127) But Hazel has not quit doing it. He accuses himself of being unclean, and continues with his mortifications: walking on stones, wrapped in barbed wire, and paying for his terrible deeds. He dies, finally, from sickness and at the hands of the police, who hit him over the head with a billy club to ensure they'll have no trouble with him.

It seems a horrible ending, and it would be in a world without God or salvation, but we must not take hold of that wrong horror. The horror in *Wise Blood* is not that Hazel suffers and dies; the horror is that the world has turned its back on its Savior. The horror is Enoch Emery's refusal to be anything but an ape, dressed in an ape costume and posing as Gonga, the ape movie star: unevolved, unredeemed, stupid, and unloved. The horror is that this troupe of loveless characters *will* not see as well as the blind man can see, and so their sins remain. But the horrors depicted in this novel are not total or despairing. There *is* redemption in *Wise Blood*. Certainly Hazel has found it.

After he dies in the back of the patrol car and is returned to Mrs. Flood's place, she welcomes his dead corpse with an announcement: "'Well, Mr. Motes, I see you've come home!'" Of course he has found his heavenly home, but the landlady isn't presuming that. She's just happy to have him and his steady government paycheck back in her possession! And yet there is something stirring in the heart of Mrs. Flood. Like the widow in the gospel story who has lost a coin of great value and searches her whole house to find it, Mrs. Flood acutely senses the loss of something vital, and she suspects that the treasure lies somewhere nearby. She intuits that there is more to Hazel Motes than a prompt paying boarder; somewhere in the vacant sockets of his eyes it seems to lurk. She sees this something as a pin point of light in a dark tunnel, "like the star on Christmas cards." (*Wise Blood, CW,*123) And what does that star, that point of light, point to but Jesus Christ, her redeemer?

She sat staring, with her eyes shut, into his eyes, and it felt as if she had finally got to the beginning of something she couldn't begin, and she saw him moving farther and farther away, farther and farther into the darkness until he was the pin point of light. (*Wise Blood, CW*, 131)

With these closing words we are left to believe that there is still hope for Mrs. Flood, that it isn't too late, and that Hazel Motes will be her guide, Christ's ambassador, and the instrument of her salvation.

In one of the finer critical works on Flannery O'Connor, Richard Giannone writes:

> Mrs. Flood's death vigil thus recapitulates the mystery of guilt and love in *Wise Blood*. We feel guilty because we are guilty. Struggle and sorrow are the debts one person owes to another. Guilt in this economy is negative in word only, and then only because our modern dread makes us think that a life without remorse is desirable. *Wise Blood* dramatizes culpability as both personal and collective. At a time when humanity seeks ways to deny and remove guilt, Flannery O'Connor redirects the reader to see the value of guilt. For O'Connor, it is the salutary burden out of which humanity recovers the humanness lost in sin. Contentment blinds O'Connor's characters to the wonder that sorrow seeks out. Guilt reveals to Hazel the abyss of his insufficiency, which serves as God's opportunity to draw Hazel closer. Guilt exposes Mrs. Flood to the empty place she inhabits. This emptiness must be uncovered before the divine can fill it. Guilt, then, prepares a way to God.[14]

We have reviewed the concept of the fall in both Camus' *The Fall* and Flannery O'Connor's *Wise Blood*. Both deal with the critical need to see reality as it is, especially when that reality is populated by flawed people and broken bonds (with God and with one another). Jean-Baptiste and Hazel Motes both recognize the fallen state of their fellows, the apes and the Gongas, but more importantly, they learn to recognize their own guilty condition. This recognition does not come easily. It requires clear vision, honesty,

14. Giannone, *Flannery O'Connor and the Mystery of Love*, 39.

and some action or event that jars them into wakefulness. Our heroes struggle to see properly, and their integrity lies in this honest attempt to see things as they are. This is the "Christian Realism" that O'Connor preached. The purpose of her art, as she describes it, is not only to see reality clearly, but to penetrate its depths and find the source of that reality, which is God. God underlies everything. God is pure being, and everything that exists participates in God's existence, and God in it. This is an understanding of God that is quite different from the transcendent, apophatic notion that God is totally "other," far removed from creation and largely unknowable. It is a sacramental aesthetic, and it is what O'Connor and others will work to see and express in their sacramental art.

In *My Dinner With André*, Wallace Shawn's 1981 film depicting a dinner conversation between two artists, Wallace (the playwright) asks his theatre friend, André, just how a writer can possibly get an audience to "wake up" and see things properly (one might mentally insert "sacramentally"). Does a person have to be taken to Mount Everest in order to experience what is real? Then what is an artist to do? Because not everyone can be taken to Mount Everest, obviously.

> But I mean, the main thing, André, is, why do we require a trip to Mount Everest in order to be able to perceive one moment of reality? Is Mount Everest more real than New York? Isn't New York real? I mean, I think if you could become fully aware of what existed in the cigar store next door to this restaurant, it would blow your brains out. I mean, isn't there just as much reality to be perceived in a cigar store as there is on Mount Everest? What do you think?[15]

André (the theatre director), responds by asserting "yes!" you do have to involve the audience in something akin to being buried alive, or some strange experience on Mount Everest; because the problem today is that people *can't see* the cigar store any more. We are too jaded, too spoiled, too blind. So the shock event of

15. Shawn and Gregory, *My Dinner With André*, 88–91.

any story—the Mount Everest experience, if you will—is needed in art as well as in life. Suffering has value. Even violence, O'Connor would assert, prepares the way for grace. Not because violence is good, not at all, but because it is *confounded* by the good; and because it awakens the wounded to a reality they could not otherwise see.

O'Conner writes: "My subject in fiction is the action of grace in territory held largely by the devil."[16] The devil has a role to play in God's salvific plan, and in ways that remain a mystery. Without some significant event there would be no story, at least not a Catholic story. Without the action of grace that rushes in on the heels of crisis there would be no essential change in the characters. For Jean-Baptiste, this key event is the suicide of the woman who leapt from the bridge, and his own sin of omission in not trying to save her. For Hazel Motes, it is the direct action of murder and the subsequent destruction of his church. Each recognizes his guilt in the death of these people, and each attempts to make amends, to confess, to atone and do penance. And while Jean-Baptiste refuses the grace that is fluttering at every window, Hazel Motes seeks it out. Jean-Baptiste's public confession may impact those he meets at *Mexico City*—since he can accuse them of sinfulness, too—but his judgment upon them will not save them. Hazel's confession, penance, acceptance, and new vision move Mrs. Flood to look for Christ in his burnt out eyes where the Lord, who will be her salvation, awaits. That is the difference.

When Albert Camus spoke to the Dominicans at the Monastery of Latour-Maubourg, he told them that the world needs courageous Christians. "Hence I shall not, as far as I am concerned, try to pass myself off as a Christian in your presence. I share with you the same revulsion from evil. But I do not share your hope . . ."[17]

Here, too, is the evidence.

---

16. Fitzgerald, *Flannery O'Connor, Mystery and Manners*, 118.

17. Camus, "The Unbeliever and Christians," 70-71.

5. The Dilemma of Sight in Annie Dillard's *Pilgrim at Tinker Creek*

Pilgrim at Tinker Creek

THERE IS ONE MORE literary work to explore with regard to the fall and this business of seeing clearly. Perhaps enough has been said, but I would contend, not yet; not quite. This will be something of a side-step, but an important one, I think. In *Pilgrim at Tinker Creek,* Annie Dillard presents us with a very immediate and rather ancient dilemma which we really should consider.

    Pilgrim at Tinker Creek is one of Dillard's earliest works. Winner of the Pulitzer Prize for General Non-Fiction in 1975, it has been compared to *Walden's Pond* as a perceptive collection of reflective prose penned by a solitary, cabin-dwelling student of nature and the divine.[1]

    In the first chapter, "Heaven and Earth in Jest," Dillard relates an incident that impressed and horrified her; an event that has never faded from her thoughts:

> A couple of summers ago I was walking along the edge
> of the island to see what I could see. . . . Frogs were flying
> all around me. At the end of the island I noticed a small

---

1. All of this is true. It is a tremendous work of literature and will survive the ages. But it is a substantial work, and merits a separate study, one which we cannot undertake here, apart from the dilemma that she presents for our consideration of sin and the fall. I do recommend you read it in its entirety. We will take a close look at Dillard's *Holy the Firm* further on in this study.

green frog. He was exactly half in and half out of the water, looking like a schematic diagram of an amphibian,
and he didn't jump.
   He didn't jump; I crept closer. At last I knelt on the
island's winterkilled grass, lost, dumbstruck, staring at
the frog in the creek just four feet away. He was a very
small frog with wide, dull eyes. And just as I looked at
him, he slowly crumpled and began to sag. The spirit
vanished from his eyes as if snuffed. His skin emptied
and drooped; his very skull seemed to collapse and
settle like a kicked tent. He was shrinking before my
eyes like a deflating football. I watched the taut, glisten-
ing skin on his shoulders ruck, and rumple, and fall.
Soon part of his skin, formless as a pricked balloon, lay
in floating folds like bright scum on top of the water:
it was a monstrous and terrifying thing. . . . An oval
shadow hung in the water behind the drained frog; then
the shadow glided away.
   I had read about the giant water bug. . . . It seizes a
victim . . . hugs it tight, and paralyzes it with enzymes
injected during a vicious bite. That one bite is the only
bite it ever takes. Through the puncture shoot the poi-
sons that dissolve the victim's muscles and bones and
organs—all but the skin, and through it the giant water
bug sucks out the victim's body, reduced to a juice. . . . I
stood up and brushed the knees of my pants. I couldn't
catch my breath. . . .
   That it's rough out there and chancy is no surprise.
(*PTC*, 5-6)

   Flannery O'Connor tells us that the artist must take a good,
hard look at things, "to penetrate the concrete world in order to
find at its depths the image of its (divine) source, the image of
ultimate reality."[2] She entices her readers to see the stars against
"the black sky, underpinned with long silver streaks," because
when we do, we may just discover the hidden God whose hands
are forever on His works. Flannery O'Connor was a keen student
of Thomas Aquinas.

2. Fitzgerald, *Flannery O'Connor, Mystery and Manners*, 157.

Just so, Bishop Robert Barron expresses it this way:

> St. Thomas gazes at the loveliness of the world in an attitude of prayer. The world in its totality is a sort of icon of the divine beauty, a mirror in which we see reflected some of the unbearable perfection of the divine being. God engages in explosive and irrepressible creativity because he is determined to show, as fully as possible, some of the intensity of his own beauty. . . . The sacramental imagination, which sees the divine lurking in every corner of the real, is fed and strengthened by the Thomistic doctrine of creation.[3]

St. Thomas suggests that the universe mirrors the beauty of its Creator. It's a lovely idea and at the heart of our study, but do you see the problem?

Annie Dillard obliges the prayerful St. Thomas and gets down on her hands and knees, in the muck and winterkilled grass, and takes one long, arduous look at that created frog, and what she sees takes her breath away; but not because of its *beauty!* "The frog that the giant water bug sucked had, presumably, a rush of pure feeling for about a second, before its brain turned to broth. I, however, have been sapped by various strong feelings about the incident almost daily for several years." (*PTC*, 178)

In a later chapter entitled "Fecundity," she comments on the immense proliferation of life in nature, on its incredible inefficiency, and on its remarkable force. Yet, she muses, "our planet alone has death. . . . Cock Robin may die the most gruesome of slow deaths, and nature is no less pleased. . . . I cannot feel that way about your death, nor you about mine, nor either of us about the robin's. . . . We value the individual supremely, and nature values him not a whit." (*PTC*, 176)

There's more. She writes of the fourteenth century Catholic mystic, Julian of Norwich, who "cites, in the manner of the prophets, these words from God: 'See, I am God: see, I am in all things: see, I never lift my hands off my works. . . . How should anything

---

3. Barron, "Creation and Beauty."

be amiss?'" But Dillard will have none of that. "It seems," she counters, "that plenty is amiss." (*PTC*, 177)

Is St. Thomas giving us the straight dope? Is there *evil* in nature? We know that there is suffering, pain, and death in the animal world, but are these things truly *evil*? If we define evil as the absence of the good that ought to be there, then shouldn't the jungle be a bit less vile? Granted, we are not talking about moral evils, as morality is beyond the realm of beasts. Yet we know that among our fellow creatures there is cruelty and horror, and that some animals even grieve over the loss of their kin.[4] To witness this suffering is unsettling enough, but there is a deeper question. If the universe mirrors the beauty of God, what are we to make of its horrors? Why do the animals suffer? What is the Christian answer to their travail? Is it on account of our *human* original sin and banishment from Eden? Then how are we to find God's hand in His works, except blithely and blindly? Annie Dillard reduces the conundrum into this basic dilemma: Either "the world my mother is a monster" or "I myself am a freak." Perhaps something is wrong with *us*, that we should suffer so in our emotions.

Artists and theologians have tried to provide answers to this dilemma for centuries. It is akin to the whole problem of evil. The Hasidic tradition in Judaism suggests that everything in creation is fractured, and God uses these gaps to spark and flare out from every broken vessel. Dillard seems to be suggesting (and she's not the first) that the fall was not just the fall of mankind, but that nature *itself* is fallen. She writes: "That something is everywhere and always amiss is part of the very stuff of creation. . . . The terms are clear. If you want to live, you have to die." (*PTC*, 180-81) "I am a frayed and nibbled survivor in a fallen world. . . . " (*PTC*, 242)

Yet, St. Thomas did not believe that creation fell with the fall of man. And while he saw that beauty in nature reflects something of its Creator, it would not necessarily follow that the grosser aspects in nature are, in the same way, a reflection of God. St. Thomas explains it thus:

4. Safina, *Beyond Words: What Animals Think and Feel.*

. . . it is more appropriate to say that the creature is like God than vice versa. For one thing is like another when it has the same quality or form. But since what is in God perfectly is present in other things by way of an imperfect participation, whatever they are alike in belongs to God absolutely, but not so to the creature. And so the creature possesses what belongs to God and is rightly said, therefore, to be like God. But we cannot also say that God has what belongs to his creature, and so neither is it appropriate to say that God is like his creature; as we do not say that a man is like his portrait, even though we state that his portrait is like him.[5]

It is God's good freedom to create a world which still bears the mark (in beauty, in freedom, in justice) of a perfect Creator.

The belief that nature fell as a result of the fall of humankind in the Garden of Eden remains, however, an influential part of our Christian tradition. The idea was best expressed by Origen of Alexandria (185-254 AD) in the third century.

Origen of Alexandria

According to Origen, humanity was close to God prior to the fall, but then our love for God diminished. This falling out of love occurred prior to the material universe, and our cosmos is the direct result of our fall from an earlier state of holiness, a fall that is shared by all beings. Since Origen is proposing a state of pre-existent perfection, we might recognize the influence of Plato's thought on his thesis, as well as the influence of the Scriptural story of a lost paradise in Genesis.

Origen claimed that creation will return to God and be reabsorbed into God when redemption is complete. This restoration, or *apokatastasis pantōn*, includes the whole creation, beasts as well as angels, and not just human beings. Origen's assertion that all will be saved (and not only the elect!) was later challenged

---

5. Clark, *Thomas Aquinas, An Aquinas Reader*, 136.

as heretical, since he included Satan and the redemption of hell itself.[6] Still, Origen was not theorizing against Scripture. St. Luke, himself a Greek, writes of "Jesus, whom heaven must receive until the times of universal restoration *(apokatastasis)* of which God spoke through the mouth of his holy prophets from of old."[7] St. Paul, who was also familiar with Plato's teachings, describes something resembling this restoration in his letter to the Romans:

> For creation awaits with eager expectation the revelation of the children of God; for creation was made subject to futility, not of its own accord but because of the one who subjected it, in hope that creation itself would be set free from slavery to corruption and share in the glorious freedom of the children of God. We know that all of creation is groaning in labor pains even until now; . . .[8]

Origen's works are complex, nuanced, and disputed; even today. Whether his writings were ever explicitly condemned is also a topic of debate. But it is important that we recognize how influential his works have been on Christian thinkers. The Catechism of the Catholic Church diplomatically states that "Because of man, creation is now subject 'to its bondage to decay.'"[9] This is an echo of Origen's proposal and St. Paul's assertion that nature is subjected to death because of our human disobedience.

What we should take from this sidetrack (and it is a sidetrack) is a second look at St. Thomas' doctrine of creation. There is beauty in nature, yes—the trickling stream glistens over sparkly stones—but if we accept the idea that creation mirrors the glory of God, as the sacramental imagination asserts, then we must also consider the underside of the rock. "Go into the gaps," Annie Dillard goads us, there's much more going on.

6. Second Council of Constantinople, 553 AD. Ironically, this belief may have laid the foundation for the Catholic Church's doctrine on Purgatory.

7. Acts 3:20–21.

8. Romans 8:19.

9. *Catechism of the Catholic Church*, 400.

It is so self-conscious, so apparently moral, simply to step
aside from the gaps where the creeks and winds pour
down, saying, I never merited this grace, quite rightly,
and then to sulk along the rest of your days on the edge
of rage. I won't have it. The world is wilder than that in all
directions, more dangerous and bitter, more extravagant
and bright. (*PTC*, 268)

What is the legacy of the fall, as seen so far? We note that
things fall apart, that something is wrong, and that suffering and
death are real. We can intuit, too, that it really shouldn't be this
way. We are all eating and eaten; we wake in blood, we live on
death, and God knows, it's chancy out there.

And yet . . . *"The world is charged with the grandeur of God!"*

6. The Poetry of Incarnation in Gerard Manley Hopkins and Thomas Merton

Gerard Manley Hopkins (1844–1889)

THERE ARE FEW PLACES more dear or more sacramental than the interior landscape of a poem by Gerard Manley Hopkins. A nineteenth century Jesuit priest and convert, Hopkins learned a way of seeing that is extraordinarily deep, intimate, pure, and extravagant. He coined the word "inscape," what we see when we ponder the close interior of things; that spark of God that permeates being because God is Being. He saw the beauty of nature that St. Thomas raised up in grace as a pool reflecting God's own grand Nature, and manages to put into words and rhyme and rhythm that mystical vision.

"God's Grandeur"

The world is charged with the grandeur of God.
    It will flame out, like shining from shook foil;
    It gathers to a greatness, like the ooze of oil
Crushed. Why do men then now not reck his rod?
Generations have trod, have trod, have trod;
    And all is seared with trade; bleared, smeared with toil;
    And wears man's smudge and shares man's smell: the soil
Is bare now, nor can foot feel, being shod.

And for all this, nature is never spent;
   There lives the dearest freshness deep down things;
And though the last lights off the black West went
   Oh, morning, at the brown brink eastward, springs—
Because the Holy Ghost over the bent
   World broods with warm breast and with ah! bright wings.
(Poems, 26)

The world is charged with God! Filled to the brim, oozing out, overflowed and flaming. And for all our human toil and our human sins, Hopkins tells us, "nature is never spent." Look at the dearest, freshness, the deep down living things. Though there is darkness, and we know the darkness will come, still the morning will spring. Because the Holy Ghost continues to love us into existence, bent over creation, comforting, warm, and glorious.

The scales tip and teeter. We have Jean-Baptiste, judged and judging our human failings. We have Hazel Motes, seeing at last his own blasphemy and murderous crimes, and burning out his eyes. We have Annie Dillard, game for a closer look, willing to go into the gaps and gawk.

The scales tip again, and now here is Hopkins, who knows the weight of feathers. The angle has changed. Our perspective shifts. We are juxtaposed, wild and in all directions. Something or someone has intruded into our story!

"The Windhover: *To Christ Our Lord*"

I caught this morning morning's minion, king-
   dom of daylight's dauphin, dapple-dawn-drawn Falcon,
      in his riding
   Of the rolling level underneath him steady air, and striding
High there, how he rung upon the rein of a wimpling wing
In his ecstasy! then off, off forth on swing,
   As a skate's heel sweeps smooth on a bow-bend: the hurl
      and gliding
   Rebuffed the big wind. My heart in hiding
Stirred for a bird,—the achieve of; the mastery of the thing!

Brute beauty and valour and act, oh, air, pride, plume, here
Buckle! AND the fire that breaks from thee then, a billion
Times told lovelier, more dangerous, O my chevalier!

No wonder of it: shéer plód makes plough down sillion
Shine, and blue-bleak embers, ah my dear,
Fall, gall themselves, and gash gold-vermillion.

(Poems, 31)

Hopkins gazes at a falcon with its wings outstretched, arcing
and rebuffing the big wind with masterful grace. The poem is dedicated "To Christ Our Lord" and Hopkins likens the falcon to our
Lord, whose beauty and fire is "a billion Times told lovelier, more
dangerous, O my chevalier!" But the pivotal point comes when all
of this beauty in brute nature, and in the nature of Jesus Christ,
here "Buckle! AND . . . " Christ's human and divine nature come
together (buckle, as in binding, God to man—the Incarnation)
and break (buckle, as in breaking—our Lord broken on the cross);
and now the fire of Christ's love breaks open to reveal his hidden,
majestic glory. "No wonder of it . . . " When a plow breaks the dull
soil, the curl of earth that peels away shines from the cut of the
blade; and when blue-bleak embers fall into the coals, they gash
open like the wounds of Christ, and reveal the gold-vermillion of
an unspeakable splendor.

The Incarnation

Hebrew Scripture reveals that our God is a Creator God, and we
are made in God's image. St. Thomas invites us to marvel over a
God who is Pure Being, lacking nothing, and is therefore the very
definition of goodness. When goodness gives itself to creation
as an expression of its own pure nature, we discover ourselves as
participants in an exquisite relationship of being. Is it any wonder,
then, that God should give Himself in the person of Jesus Christ,
the Second Person of the Trinity, who is the Incarnation?

What is meant by "Incarnation" in this sense? The term was defined at the first ecumenical Council of Nicaea in 325, that Jesus' nature is both divine and human, not in two parts, but in its entirety. The liturgy speaks of God "who humbled himself to share in our humanity." It is customary for Catholics to bow down in homage when we pray the creed: "by the Holy Spirit (he) was incarnate of the Virgin Mary and became man." To become incarnate is to become enfleshed.

The Incarnation is *the sacramental event* in human history. It is the focal point that changes everything. It is certainly at the center of our Christian faith.

Edward Schillebeeckx, OP, expands on St. Thomas' claim that the Incarnation is not only necessary for our redemption, it is *the point* of our very existence. "Man is created for Christ."[1] As we read in the chapter on the sacraments, Christ is the very Sacrament of God. Jesus Christ, the Second Person of the Holy Trinity, by taking on human form and by his redemptive actions, reveals something of the divine relationship of love between God the Father and God the Son. When the apostle Philip said to Jesus "Master, show us the Father," Jesus responds (with something sounding like exasperation): "Have I been with you for so long a time and you still do not know me, Philip? Whoever has seen me has seen the Father."[2]

Christ's redemptive deeds (in his life, death, resurrection, and ascension) are the outward, human, bodily signs of a divine, relational love that is absolute generosity. And these actions are eternal and enduring in the sacraments of the church because they are the actions of God.

St. Gregory of Nyssa gives us this to ponder:

> Sick, our nature demanded to be healed; fallen, to be raised up; dead, to rise again. We had lost the possession of the good; it was necessary for it to be given back to us. Closed in darkness, it was necessary to bring us the light; captives, we awaited a Savior; prisoners, help; slaves, a

---

1. Schillebeeckx, *Christ the Sacrament of Encounter with God,* 7, footnote 1.
2. John 14:9-11.

liberator. Are these things insignificant? Did they not move God to descend to human nature and visit it since humanity was in so miserable and unhappy a state?[3]

Within the Lenten liturgy, we cry "Oh, Happy Fault!" that the fall of Adam has brought about the Incarnation of God. John Milton, at the end of his magnificent work, *Paradise Lost,* has Adam exclaiming with joy upon seeing the future of his progeny and God's salvific plan: that God will enter into creation and redeem us through the sacrifice of Jesus Christ.

"O Goodness infinite, Goodness immense!
That all this good of evil shall produce,
And evil turn to good—more wonderful
Than that which by creation first brought forth
Light out of darkness!"[4]

The Incarnation is more wonderful than creation itself! That is something we might want to prayerfully ponder next Christmas.

Thomas Merton's "Hagia Sophia"

Thomas Merton was the quintessential twentieth-century man. He was born in France in 1915 while World War I raged, and he died in Asia in 1968 at the height of the Vietnam War. Merton was a brilliant and worldly young man who studied literature and languages at Cambridge and then Columbia University, preparing for a career in diplomacy. He converted to Catholicism and was baptized into the Catholic faith in 1938. After graduating from Columbia in 1939, he taught literature at St. Bonaventure College for a short time and then entered a Trappist monastery in Kentucky in 1941.

Though he expected a cloistered life to be a life of prayer and physical labor, Merton was told by his superiors that he must also use his gifts and write; and he was a prolific writer. His

---

3. *Catechism of the Catholic Church,* 457.

4. Milton, *Paradise Lost,* Book 12, lines 469-72, 299.

autobiography, *The Seven Storey Mountain*, became a national bestseller, but he also wrote extensively on contemplative prayer, mysticism, war, peace, and racial justice.

Thomas Merton was a monk, a priest, and a poet. And one of the most beautiful poetic works on the Incarnation is Merton's "Hagia Sophia." It begins:

> There is in all visible things an invisible fecundity, a dimmed light, a meek namelessness, a hidden whole-ness. This mysterious Unity and Integrity is Wisdom, the Mother of all, *Natura naturans*. There is in all things an inexhaustible sweetness and purity, a silence that is a fount of action and joy. It rises up in wordless gentle-ness and flows out to me from the unseen roots of all created being, welcoming me tenderly, saluting me with indescribable humility. This is at once my own being, my own nature, and the Gift of my Creator's Thought and Art within me, speaking as Hagia Sophia, speaking as my sister, Wisdom. ("Hagia Sophia," 61)

Here again we experience the "inscape" of deep-down splen-dor; that interior spark, that point of light, that name of God in our own name. Merton's prose poem endeavors to reach the very heart and source of the Incarnation. He reveals this feminine heart as Holy Wisdom who is in all things, like the air receiving the sun-light; and the source as God the Father.

Who is Hagia Sophia? Is she a person, a deity, or a metaphor? Do we even know? Does Merton know? He really does not attempt to analyze or explain her being. Instead, he gives us image after image, sign upon sign, and layer upon layer; allowing us to form our own nagging insight into this inexpressible reality, one that we might not otherwise have imagined. He provides a litany of similes in his endeavor to describe her: She is *like* the Virgin Mary. She is *like* Eve. She is *like* the Mother of all. He even suggests that Sophia is Ousia: Is *Being*. He leans toward the notion that she is of the Trinity, but wisely backs away. No, she is "a meek nameless-ness," a child playing before the Father. What she gives to God is delight and joy in His creation. What she gives to the world is the Incarnation.

She awakens the sleeping and helpless man with tenderness, waking him into being. He is born "strong at the voice of mercy." Now she, Sophia, diffuses the midday Light of God, making God's face bearable for the waking man to see; and then to recognize that it is the human face of Christ. "God enters without publicity into the city of rapacious men."

> The shadows fall. The stars appear. The birds begin to sleep. . . . A vagrant, a destitute wanderer with dusty feet, finds his way down a new road. A homeless God, lost in the night . . . lies down in desolation under the sweet stars of the world and entrusts Himself to sleep. ("Hagia Sophia," 68–69)

Moses was blessed to see the back of God from the gaps, as a presence moving quickly past him. But Sophia's gift to us is the participation of God in creation; a gift greater than our own existence. She awakens the sleeping man into consciousness; she draws Adam into existence; she is the "unseen pivot of all nature." But it is in Mary, in Mary's wise answer, that Sophia is known. She is not "a creator and not a redeemer, but perfect creature, perfectly redeemed." She "sets upon the Second Person, the Logos, a crown which is His Human Nature." Not a crown glorious—as we might expect of the Son begotten of the Father—but a crown weak, helpless and poor; and sends Him forth (with dusty feet!) "in His mission of inexpressible mercy, to die for us on the Cross." ("Hagia Sophia," 68)

What is the Legacy of the Incarnation?

The Incarnation is the focal point of the Christian faith. Milton remarks (through Adam's vision) that this divine action is far greater than creation itself, and justifiably so. God not only enters into our human history, He has left us a legacy of salvation which makes us "come to share in the divine nature."[5]

In practical terms of morality and governance, the church teaches that our human rights flow from this divine source and are grounded in human sanctity. Therefore, our moral codes, our virtues, and the just laws that we enact all rest upon the foundation of human dignity. Without this grounding we are subject to raw power; with it, we are made holy.

In spiritual terms, the Incarnation grants us the graces which Christ purchased by his sacrificial act. Through his teachings, Jesus reveals the nature of God to us; that God is a relationship of three Persons (the Holy Trinity) and that God is love. He establishes the church on earth and institutes the sacraments to redirect us in our relationship to God and to aid us with grace in our struggle to live holy lives. Among these gifts is the greatest sacrament of all, the Holy Eucharist, to feed us with his sacred body and blood, incarnate in the bread and wine, as food for our journey. In his death on the cross Jesus redeems us from sin and opens the gates of heaven that we might come to share in his divinity. After his resurrection, Jesus sends the gift of the Holy Spirit to help guide the church in her mission to safeguard Christ's teachings, administer the sacraments, and to make the Sacrament of God, who is Christ, known to all nations.

Merton's Diary

In 1963, coming home from a visit to the hospital in Louisville, Thomas Merton experienced a sudden moment of insight that he later retells in his journal. It was a moment of perfect clarity; as if he were peering at the inner sanctity of every person on the street.

> In Louisville, at the corner of Fourth and Walnut, in the center of the shopping district, I was suddenly overwhelmed with the realization that I loved all those people, that they were mine and I theirs, that we could

5. 2 Peter 1:4.

not be alien to one another even though we were total strangers. It was like waking from a dream of separateness. . . . it was as if I suddenly saw the secret beauty of their hearts, the depths of their hearts where neither sin nor desire nor self-knowledge can reach, the core of their reality, the person that each one is in God's eyes.[6]

Contrast this with Taulkinham and Enoch's complaint: "Only objection I got to Taulkinham is there's too many people on the streets. . . . Look like all they want to do is knock you down." (*Wise Blood*, 23) Why the contrast? What has happened, that Merton should experience his city and people so differently? Here is a contemplative, cloistered in his Trappist monastery, and mingling among the people of his city on a rare outing. His is a different vision, perhaps because of his life of prayer and sacrifice and worship. Still, his ability to see the people as God sees them is a vision, he insists, that is *pure gift* and not something earned. His life's work will be to teach others a little of what he has learned.

If only they could all see themselves as they really *are*. If only we could see each other that way all the time. There would be no more war, no more hatred, no more cruelty, no more greed. . . . But this cannot be *seen*, only believed and "understood" by a peculiar gift. . . . At the center of our being is a point of nothingness which is untouched by sin and by illusion, a point of pure truth, a point or spark which belongs entirely to God, which is never at our disposal, from which God disposes of our lives, which is inaccessible to the fantasies of our own mind or the brutalities of our own will. This little point of nothingness and of *absolute poverty* is the pure glory of God in us. . . . It is like a pure diamond, blazing with the invisible light of heaven. It is in everybody, and if we could see it we would see these billions of points of light coming together in the face and blaze of a sun that would make all the darkness and cruelty of life vanish completely. . . .

6. Merton, *Conjectures of a Guilty Bystander*, 140-42.

I have no program for this seeing. It is only given. But the
gate of heaven is everywhere.[7]

One might think that O'Connor borrowed from Merton's
journal entry when she wrote *Wise Blood* and described, through
Mrs. Flood, the point of light in Hazel's hollow sockets; a pin point
that drew her further into the mystery of Hazel's holiness. But the
timing of the writings makes this impossible. It is more likely that
Thomas Merton borrowed from O'Connor's novel, which was
written ten years earlier, or that they both, perhaps, had the same
vision and expressed it in very similar language, because we are
called to see one another as God sees us, with eyes of love and
compassion. This is the meaning behind "love thy neighbor as thy-
self," and what is commanded of us as a holy people.

7. Ibid., 142.

7. The Incarnation and Grace in Flannery O'Connor's "Parker's Back" and "Revelation"

Kafka's "In the Penal Colony" and the Sanctity of Human Life

"Where there is no vision, the people perish."

Proverbs 29:19

WITHOUT SOME NOTION OF the sanctity of life, we govern by force and even terror. This dreadful state is well expressed in Franz Kafka's short story, "In the Penal Colony," which we will look at next as another brief aside.

"In the Penal Colony" tells a nightmarish tale about a fantastic machine, invented by clever men to enact a final judgment upon condemned prisoners. Here, a nameless officer takes a nameless explorer on a tour of some nameless compound in order to show this visitor his most prized instrument. He describes the thing in great detail. It is a massive machine with a giant wheel, dials, needles and arms, and a grisly harrow with teeth. There is a spindle that turns the living, naked body of a condemned man on an apparatus that suspends him over a pit. This monstrosity makes Camus's torture box, the "little-ease," seem tame!

The great machine inscribes—with fantastic embellishment of the text—the crimes of the condemned man into his flesh, slowly, with needles. "It takes twelve hours," the proud officer tells his guest, to complete its task. At first, the gagged prisoner is unaware of the inscription. He is not told his crimes or his sentence. "He will learn it in his body," the officer explains. When the machine goes to work inscribing the offences, he only feels the pain of the needles as they begin to dig deeper. Cotton swabs mechanically clear away the blood. The man's body is turned. New inscriptions begin on the other side of him. His ordeal is torturous. For hours he endures it. Then the felt gag is removed, "because the man has no more strength to scream." Rice pudding is provided for him in an "electrically-heated bowl" that he can lap at with his tongue when his head is turned in that direction. None refuse it, until the sixth hour when the condemned lose their desire for food. The officer explains it this way:

> But how quiet he grows at just about the sixth hour!
> Enlightenment comes to the most dull-witted. It be-
> gins around the eyes. From there it radiates. A moment
> that might tempt one to get under the Harrow oneself.
> Nothing more happens than that the man begins to
> understand the inscription, he purses his mouth as if he
> were listening. . . . By that time the Harrow has pierced
> him quite through and casts him into the pit, where he
> pitches down upon the blood and water and the cotton
> wool. Then the judgment has been fulfilled, and we, the
> soldier and I, bury him.[1]

The moment of truth for the condemned man is when he realizes that the needles are inscribing his crimes into his flesh, and that he is being slowly tortured to death by his own sins. (It is stories such as these that give "Kafkaesque" its grisly meaning!)

The penal colony itself is terrifying, and the great machine is as ghastly as any instrument of torture that human beings can imagine. When it comes to condemnation, Jean-Baptiste knew the possibilities of man's inhumanity. "Don't wait for the Last Judgment," he warns his confessor, "it takes place every day." (*The Fall*, 111)

So what are we to make of this gruesome tale of punishment? It goes far beyond the grotesque ghost stories of Edgar Allen Poe, or the existential wasteland of Jean-Paul Sartre's works. As for our

1. Kafka, "In the Penal Colony," 204.

sacramental literature, it seems to work directly against the very event that drives the story forward, that "action of grace" that awakens the characters to a deeper reality. The condemned man does have an epiphany of a kind, when he finally recognizes the meaning of the text that is inscribed in his flesh, but this is an action of force not grace. The punishment is worked, but it is pure cruelty, with no hope of redemption.

Do you think "In the Penal Colony" is a sacramental tale? Oh, no, not at all! It is, at least at its own level, the complete *opposite* of sacramental literature. Kafka's horror is exactly the horror that he depicts. There is no underlying grace; there is only the clear presentation of evil in a mechanized, inhuman, totalitarian state, where God is clearly absent; a void where the good ought to be. The malevolence is plain, highly detailed, and presented in the raw for all to see. One's guilt will be determined by other men, and them alone; and one's punishment will be determined by other men, and them alone. Those in power will build great instruments of torture—because they can, and they know how—and the condemned will get exactly what the powerful say they deserve. The extent to which one man can punish another is limited only by human invention, not by moral conscience, because there can be no such thing as moral conscience in a godless universe.

"In the Penal Colony" is an allegorical tale with a complex message hidden beneath the surface story, but that hidden message bears no resemblance to hope or redemption or underlying grace. It is a gruesome and nihilistic message, one that depicts moral relativism at its most extreme and absurd end. It is Taulkinham without the hope of Jesus. It is hell on earth; a nightmare from which one never wakes.

Kafka's "In the Penal Colony" is critiqued alongside our sacramental literature to show the *contrast* between a humanity that is fallen and a humanity without God. This contrast, I hope, will help us understand how *The Fall* and *Wise Blood,* though different from one another, still have a crucial element in common; and how each opposes the grim, existential anxiety that is evoked by Kafka's chilling tale. This anxiety is rooted in our innate understanding that human judgment, unchecked by moral law, can (and has, and will) inflict a tremendous blow against human life and human dignity. Even when society employs gentler means than the one purposed by Kafka's machine, we should recognize that any assault against human life is a betrayal of our dignity. Punishment devoid of justice is evil. It is, for us, a betrayal of the Incarnation of Christ. From a sacramental perspective (which was not Kafka's, though he was certainly insightful), such punishment is thoroughly demonic and exists as pure terror.[2]

Flannery O'Connor astutely identifies this terror:

> In the absence of this faith now, we govern by tenderness. It is a tenderness which, long since cut off from the person of Christ, is wrapped in theory. When tenderness is detached from the source of tenderness, its logical outcome is terror. It ends in forced labor camps and in the fumes of the gas chamber.[3]

"In the Penal Colony" manifests this tenderness by the unexpected bowl of rice pudding that is given to the tortured man (and kept warm for him) when he is too weak to scream. At this moment the officer is so moved by the prisoner's calamity that he considers lying down beside him. It is not unlike the sponge of sour wine that was hoisted up to the lips of Jesus, when he cried out in anguish from the cross.

We can find examples of this distorted tenderness in our own world, well beyond the harmless diction of a story:

- There is the tragedy of abortion, claiming that "every child should be wanted" and so removing the child.

2. Franz Kafka was born in Prague in 1883 and died in 1924, before the start of WWII and Hitler's Holocaust. Yet his writings foreshadow a great tragedy awaiting Europe and his own Jewish people. "In the Penal Colony" was written in 1914, prior even to WWI, but it was revised after the Great War. Kafka's premonition of the totalitarian state is certainly remarkable, though it may be attributed to the German militarism that permeated the culture during his short life time.

3. O'Connor, "Introduction to A Memoir of Mary Ann," *Collected Works,* 830-31.

- There is the antiseptic swab over the vein of the condemned man, who awaits the executioner's lethal injection.

- Torture is redefined as "enhanced interrogation," while doctors hover near the victim to ensure his survival.

- We tally the death of innocent civilians as "collateral damage."

- We "assist" with another's "suicide."

- We speak of nuclear weaponry as "peaceful deterrence."

These are not the ways of justice or the moral law, and it is the Catholic belief that Christ's Incarnation, which sanctifies human life, must direct the church to reject—and always reject—these social evils. Quite so, for without the foundation of human dignity, upon what would we base our human rights? Social contracts change as readily as governments. Without Christ's commandment to love our enemies, and without the belief that God established us with a dignity that partakes in the divine life of Christ, our tender effort to administer justice so easily distorts and morphs into terror.

Flannery O'Connor's short story, "The Lame Shall Enter First," makes this morphing of divine justice excruciatingly evident. It recounts the well-intentioned actions of a widowed counselor who tries to reform a homeless, delinquent teen by taking him into his home. While he tends to the rehabilitation of the older boy, he tragically ignores the anguish of his own young son, who is still mourning the death of his mother. The father, who does not believe in God or immortality, has no comfort to give his grieving child. He is too honest to relay a fable that he himself cannot believe, and he wants his childish boy to grow up and accept the fact that death is the end of existence. All he can give the boy is the stark comfort that his dead mother no longer exists. So she is not unhappy, "she just isn't." The boy wails and vomits out this comfort food. Goodness, and truth, and kindness all twist in unexpected turmoil in this story, until the reader begins to realize that there is a tender, hidden terror in these relationships; one that should not be ignored. With pointed realism, O'Connor will make the logical outcome of this well-meaning tenderness—*divorced from its divine source*—seen for what it is, and then it will be "too late."

After Franz Kafka's most un-sacramental tale, we will next turn to Flannery O'Connor's "Parker's Back." The two are strangely linked, perhaps intentionally so, since both deal explicitly with the very flesh of our human bodies and their value. In Kafka's nightmare, only the powerful can determine the use and value of human life. In O'Connor's sacramental tale, and perhaps as a response to Kafka, the human body is graphically shown to be the instrument through which our salvation is achieved.

"Parker's Back"

Of all the stories written by Flannery O'Connor, I am most fond of "Parker's Back." I consider "Revelation" her finest work, to the point of perfection, but "Parker's Back" has a special place in my heart, perhaps because it was her last story and it is not as polished as the others. It has a certain raw, sour, bite to it that makes O. E. Parker that much more endearing, at least to me. ("Aw shut your mouth for a change.") And O'Connor was still making small edits to the text when she died in the hospital, which adds some intensity to the heart-punch one feels at the end of it.

"Parker's Back" is a story about heresy. Specifically, it is a story that counters the Docetist heresy—which taught that human beings can worship God only in spirit, and that the material world is evil—with the sacramental view that reveals God at work and embedded in the material world.[4]

O. E. Parker, O'Connor's lusty protagonist, is an impetuous young man who, over the course of his life, has managed to cover his body in tattoos. And since the Docetists believed that human

4. Flannery O'Connor herself describes Sarah Ruth's heresy as "Manichean." However, for the sake of historical accuracy, it comes much closer to Docetism, which was a heresy that proclaimed the material world as evil and the spiritual world as good. Manichaeism was a religion in its own right and less a "heresy" in the proper sense of the word. (See: *Mystery and Manners*, 68, and *The Habit of Being*, 594.)

flesh is evil and must be transcended, Parker's colorful collision with similar minded believers centers the story.

His backwoods wife, Sarah Ruth, is a staunch advocate of all things spiritual, and her home taught beliefs are based more heavily upon the laws of the Old Testament than the Good News of the New. She embraces the spirit to the point of condemning the flesh, preferring the austerity of an unworldly faith to the bloody, bodily worship of pagans (and Catholics). In addition to being against icon and color, Sarah Ruth is no beauty. Indeed, she is "plain, plain." Sharp, distrustful, hungry and thin, she has a complexion "as tight as the skin on an onion." She is suspicious of cars (and any foreign idea that might come down the road in one of them), is no cook (she "just threw food in the pot and let it boil,") and is "forever sniffing up sin." Sarah Ruth's toothless mother is only interested in the food that Parker brings by, while her father, "a Straight Gospel preacher," is away "spreading it in Florida." Sarah Ruth herself "did not smoke or dip, drink whiskey, use bad language or paint her face, and God knew some paint would have improved it, Parker thought. Her being against color, it was the more remarkable she had married him." But marry they do, and in the most comic of courtships. It is no wonder that "marriage did not change Sarah Ruth a jot." After months of miserable wedded bliss, and on account of her constant hen-pecking and shoddy meals, Parker is literally "losing flesh." The tattoo artist that Parker visits can barely recognize him. "'You've fallen off some,' he said. 'You must have been in jail.' 'Married,' Parker said. 'Oh,' said the artist." ("Parker's Back," *CW,* 666)

Sarah Ruth may be a common enough figure in a culture influenced by Puritan pilgrims, but by the same token, Parker can hardly be called a Christian, Straight Gospel or otherwise. He runs from religion the same way he runs from his family, the government, and the US Navy. He is un-churched, earthy, sensual, and self-directed. But O'Connor's sympathies are with the pagan Parker and not with the prickly Sarah Ruth. There is an interior goodness about him. He wants to please his wife, yet he can't help but be repelled by her. His attraction to Sarah Ruth is nonsensical, conflicting, and haphazard, just like his disordered life. What had most inspired him as a youngster—the tattooed man he once saw at a fair—is a botched mess on his own skin. His tattoos are amateurish and random. He is drifting without a guide and driven by his own fleshly passions, which only lead him toward that which repels him most (Sarah Ruth).

Parker's dissatisfaction with his job and his marriage reaches its height when, in a sun-soaked daze, he drives the tractor he's riding on into a tree and is thrown from it. "GOD ABOVE!" he shouts in mid-air. The tractor and tree burst into flames while Parker's shoes go flying, to burn a short distance away. Terrified and awestruck, he crawls backwards to his truck, "halfway to it he got up and began a kind of forward-bent run from which he collapsed on his knees twice." ("Parker's Back," *CW*, 665) This is holy ground, indeed; the burning bush, the empty shoes, and glimpse of God above.

The magnitude of the event propels Parker into town where he is determined to get a tattoo of God emblazoned on his back, the only empty place left on his body. When the tattoo artist asks Parker what kind of image he wants, Parker replies simply: "God." The artist is unperturbed: "Father, Son, or Spirit?" he asks, handing him a catalogue of images. ("Parker's Back," 435) Parker thumbs through the artist's book of pictures, going backwards in time (which is an amusing run through our cultural depictions of Jesus!) until he lands on a Byzantine mosaic of Christ, with "all-demanding eyes" that say to him "GO BACK." (Repent, turn around). Parker points to the image, but the artist balks, "That'll cost you plenty." Parker insists, saying he wants that image and copied just as it is. The artist concedes, "It's your funeral." ("Parker's Back," *CW*, 667)

One wonders why Flannery O'Connor would choose a tattoo to illustrate her story about Christian heresy and redemption. We recall Kafka's grisly "In the Penal Colony," where the condemned man's crimes are etched with needles into his flesh. There has to be a response to the horror of torture and a godless world that desecrates the human body. In "Parker's Back," O'Connor graphically shows, with her own set of needles, that Jesus Christ is truly embedded in our human flesh because the Word was made flesh. The Second Person of the Trinity redeems us and sanctifies us in our very bodies, and not just our nature or our souls. Timothy Radcliffe, OP, writes: "The body is central to all the major Christian doctrines. We believe that God creates our bodies and drew near to us in Jesus Christ, flesh and blood like us. Our central sacrament is the sharing of his body. . . . We are not spirits trapped in bags of flesh but corporeal beings whose communion always has a bodily foundation."[5] Catholicism is, according to Eleanor Heartney, a "sensualist" religion. As was quoted in the first chapter:

> . . . all the major mysteries of the Catholic faith—among them Christ's Incarnation, his Crucifixion and Resurrection, the Resurrection of the faithful at the end of time, and the Transubstantiation of bread and wine into Christ's body and blood during the Mass—center around the human body. Without Christ's assumption of human form, there could be no real sacrifice, and hence, no real salvation for mankind.[6]

But Parker cannot know any of this; he has no use for religion. He is only following some inner voice when he chooses the mosaic Jesus. As he has done all his life, Parker obeys whatever instinct drives him, and now the eyes of the Byzantine Christ are eyes he must obey.

When the tattoo is finished Parker leaves the shop, drinks a pint of whiskey, gets himself into a bar fight over this new tattoo, and is thrown bodily out of the tavern. He sits in the alley in a state of confusion, examining his soul. "He saw it as a spider web of facts and lies. . . ." At last he decides to go home to Sarah Ruth, who can give him some spiritual guidance. A change has come over Parker now. The incident with the burning tree, and the tattooed image of Christ in his flesh have changed him. " . . . he observed that his dissatisfaction was gone, but he felt not quite like himself. It was as if he were himself but a stranger to himself,

5. Radcliffe, OP, *What is the Point of Being a Christian?* 89-90.

6. Heartney, "Blood, Sex, and Blasphemy: The Catholic Imagination in Contemporary Art," 3.

driving into a new country though everything he saw was familiar to him." ("Parker's Back," *CW,* 672)

He arrives home only to discover that Sarah Ruth has locked him out of the house. She will not allow him back in until he tells her who he is; in other words, when he speaks his baptismal name: Obadiah [servant of God] Elihue [my God is He]. After some protest he obliges her and gives his name. Then "all at once he felt the light pouring through him, turning his spider web soul into a perfect arabesque of colors, a garden of trees and birds and beasts. . . ." ("Parker's Back," *CW,* 673) This beautiful arabesque is the visible dwelling place of God; and it should remind us of Parker's first experience with wonder at the sight of the tattooed man at the fair. Now his botched, self-directed life has achieved an order and light that is gifted by this sacramental moment. The door opens to him.

Sadly, it is only Sarah Ruth on the other side. He begins to remove his shirt to show her the tattoo. "'And you ain't going to have none of me this near morning,' she said." But Parker ignores the rebuff, turns around, and reveals to her the image of Christ. She doesn't even recognize him.

> "Another picture," Sarah Ruth growled, "I might have known . . . "
>
> "Don't just say that! *Look* at it! . . . It's him . . . God!"
>
> "God? God don't look like that!"
>
> "What do you know how he looks?" Parker moaned, "You ain't seen him."
>
> "He don't *look,*" Sarah Ruth said. "He's a spirit. No man shall see his face."
>
> "Aw listen," Parker groaned, "this is just a picture of him."
>
> "Idolatry!" Sarah Ruth screamed. "Idolatry! Enflaming yourself with idols under every green tree! I can put up with lies and vanity but I don't want no idolator in this house!" and she grabbed up the broom and began to thrash him across the shoulders with it. ("Parker's Back," *CW,* 674)

The Jewish authorities condemned Jesus for declaring his oneness with God, and for that reason—they claimed—he was flogged and put to death. Once again, and for the same reason, Jesus is beaten by those scandalized by the Incarnation; "and large welts had formed on the face of the tattooed Christ." Parker is stunned, and staggers for the door.

> She stamped the broom two or three times on the floor and went to the window and shook it out to get the taint of him off it. Still gripping it, she looked toward the pecan tree and her eyes hardened still more. There he was— who called himself Obadiah Elihue—leaning against the tree, crying like a baby. ("Parker's Back," *CW*, 674-75)

Sarah Ruth's future seems rigid and set. She may well remain exactly what she is: against color, against her own bodily nature, abstract, and in denial of human sanctity and the Word made flesh. Yet her fate is not entirely hopeless, she does carry a child in her womb, which is a fruitful sign of hope for her future. But O. E. Parker has been reborn. Imbued in his flesh is the image of his Creator, and he receives the grace that turns his soul into a perfect arabesque of color when he speaks the name he was given at his baptism; that name known only to God.[7]

Obadiah Elihue's body, his own earthly existence, is the instrument of his salvation and unity with God. This is the pivotal point. God does not redeem us in spirit. God has redeemed us through a bloody event in our human story. Obadiah Elihue may well cry "like a baby," but these are the tears of one born again; an infant turned outward and directed at last toward God.

---

7. O'Connor purposefully states that Parker was already baptized, as his full and true name "was on his baptismal record which he got at the age of a month; his mother was a Methodist." ("Parker's Back," *CW*, 662) Methodists believe in infant baptism, and in her letters O'Connor asks her correspondent about this fact, to ensure the accuracy of her story. She does this, I believe, in order to emphasize the importance of Parker's baptism and the graces he received from the sacrament, graces that are sealed for life and which gently direct him on his path to salvation.

"Revelation"

'... *mercy triumphs over judgment.*'

James 2:13

If "Parker's Back" is a story about heresy, then "Revelation" might well be described as a story about grace and the mercy of God. Both stories give us likable protagonists: earnest, well-meaning, flawed—as is any human being heir to original sin—but salvageable. Where O. E. Parker has spent his life running from religion (like Hazel Motes), Ruby Turpin has embraced it with joy and deep satisfaction. "'And wona these days I know I'll we-eara crown.'" She is a true believer in salvation, thankful, and fully aware that God has graced her life. With a theology akin to the Calvinist, Ruby Turpin's gratitude is weighed according to her many blessings. She is grateful for who she is, how she was made, the bounty of her life with her husband Claud, as well as her own demonstrated goodness, which is real. She *is* a good woman. But she is mistaken in her notion of grace and how it has been merited.

The Catholic notion of grace is defined as a gift from God; a gift of help from our fallen state and a gift that aids us in becoming holy. It is not material wealth, earthly happiness, or the contentment one feels in knowing that one is saved. It is the help God gives us in order to respond to our vocation or calling in life. The Lord beckons us to work with him to perfect our lives and he gives us the grace to do so. Through the work of the Holy Spirit, we are all able to attain eternal life because that is what God wills.

O'Connor's position on how grace works in literature can be found in the essay "On Her Own Work" where she writes:

> The action or gesture I'm talking about would have to be on the anagogical level, that is, the level which has to do with the Divine life and our participation in it. It would be a gesture that transcended any neat allegory that might have been intended, or any pat moral categories

a reader could make. It would be a gesture which some-how made contact with mystery.[8]

This action, this gesture, this contact with mystery is beautifully crafted in "Revelation." Here we have a middle aged woman—stout, pleasing, and well dressed—who enters a doctor's waiting room and engages in light conversation with the other patient patients there. She quickly sizes up the room's handful of occupants and instantly judges each according to their appearance; judgments that are none too generous. She directs her attention and conversation toward a "stylish lady" who suits her own social sphere. If one is going to base one's assessment of another person by their station in life, as if wealth and fashion were blessings from a well-pleased God, then it would naturally follow that those who have not achieved a high social status are somehow displeasing to God. This is Ruby Turpin's logic, which is perfectly reasonable, though based on a false assumption. Intuitively, Ruby is aware of this. She seems to realize that there is a problem. While lying awake at night she often would categorize the classes of people in her head in order to assure herself of her own good place, but she realizes that the categories quickly break down.

On the bottom of the heap were most colored people, not the kind she would have been if she had been one, but most of them; then next to them—not above, just away from—were the white-trash; then above them were the home-owners, and above them the home-and-land owners, to which she and Claud belonged. Above she and Claud were people with a lot of money and much bigger houses and much more land. But here the complexity of it would begin to bear in on her, for some of the people with a lot of money were common and ought to be below she and Claud and some of the people who had good blood had lost their money and had to rent and then there were colored people who owned their homes and land as well. There was a colored dentist in town who had two red Lincolns and a swimming pool and a farm with registered white-faced cattle on it. Usually by the

8. Fitzgerald, *Flannery O'Connor, Mystery and Manners*, 111.

time she had fallen asleep all the classes of people were moiling and roiling around in her head, and she would dream they were all crammed in together in a box car, being ridden off to be put in a gas oven. ("Revelation," *CW*, 636)

The gas ovens operated by those who also categorized people by race and status! But the dream does not sway her from her long-established way of seeing. It will take much more than that.

As she prattles along in the waiting room, boasting of her many blessings and the generosity of God who gave her "a little of everything," a young college student (reading a book called *Human Development* and studying at a *northern* university!) begins to make ugly faces at her.[9] This is something Ruby Turpin does not understand. "Girl, Mrs. Turpin exclaimed silently, I haven't done a thing to you!" ("Revelation," *CW*, 642) Nor have any of the others in the waiting room done a thing to Mrs. Turpin, yet they still fall victim to her own impetuous judgments! But Ruby misses this irony and her own hypocrisy, and so the ugly faces continue.

There are at least three events in "Revelation" that might count as an "action of grace." The first is an act of violence, delivered in the midst of Mrs. Turpin's exclamation of gratitude to our Lord and by the ugly college girl:

"If it's one thing I am," Mrs. Turpin said with feeling, "it's grateful. When I think who all I could have been besides myself and what all I got, a little of everything, and a good disposition besides, I just feel like shouting, 'Thank you, Jesus . . . Oh thank you, Jesus, Jesus, thank you!'" she cried aloud.

The book struck her directly over her left eye. It struck almost at the same instant that she realized the girl was about to hurl it. ("Revelation," *CW*, 644)

There is a tremendous scuffle as the girl lunges at Mrs. Turpin, digging her fingers into her throat, and shrieking. She has to be tackled to the floor and restrained. Then, from the waiting room

9. Did you catch her name? It is 'Mary Grace.' I hope you noticed this!

floor, the girl utters a fierce directive at Mrs. Turpin: "Go back to hell where you came from, you old wart hog."

After the mêlée, Mary Grace is sedated and removed by ambulance, Claud sees his doctor, and then the Turpins go home. But the girl's condemnation rends Ruby Turpin's heart. She is not in the least bit confused about it. She knows that it was delivered by God as a judgment against her.

> "I am not," she said tearfully, "a wart hog. From hell." But the denial had no force. The girl's eyes and her words, even the tone of her voice, low but clear, directed only to her, brooked no repudiation. She had been singled out for the message, though there was trash in the room to whom it might justly have been applied. . . . The tears dried. Her eyes began to burn instead with wrath. ("Revelation," *CW*, 647-48)

Ruby's indignation turns to fury. She "raised her fist and made a small stabbing motion over her chest as if she was defending her innocence to invisible guests who were like the comforters of Job, reasonable-seeming but wrong." ("Revelation," *CW*, 648) This is not the only reference to Job. Above her eye, where the book struck her, is a bruise that looked like "a miniature tornado cloud." We should remember that God answered Job out of the whirlwind.

In the natural order of things, Ruby's indignation seems justified. Why *was* this message delivered to her: a respectable, hardworking, church-going woman, who gave to anyone in need, white or black? It would be too simple to see her only as a hypocrite, or mean-spirited, or corrupt. She is most believable when she says that she is respectable and decent and good. But the mystery of God's mercy makes clear, in the teachings of Jesus whom Ruby loves, that the "last shall be first." Jesus does not bless the finest among us, but the least. And while Ruby is a clear champion of God's just judgment, she is floored—literally knocked off her feet—by God's inexplicable mercy. If only Camus had understood this! It is not judgment that we should dread, but mercy that we should hope for, because it is never too late for God's mercy.

This is expressed beautifully in the letter of St. James, which must have influenced O'Connor's story, right down to the waiting room assembly and Mrs. Turpin's directives of where people ought to sit and who there might be stylish enough to warrant her attention:

> My brothers, show no partiality as you adhere to the faith in our glorious Lord Jesus Christ. For if a man with gold rings on his fingers and in fine clothes comes into your assembly, and a poor person in shabby clothes also comes in, and you pay attention to the one wearing the fine clothes and say, "Sit here, please," while you say to the poor one, "Stand there" . . . have you not made distinctions among yourselves and become judges with evil designs? Listen, my beloved brothers. Did not God choose those who are poor in the world to be rich in faith and heirs of the kingdom that he promised to those who love him? But you dishonored the poor person. Are not the rich oppressing you? . . . If you show partiality, you commit sin . . . for the judgment is merciless to one who has not shown mercy; mercy triumphs over judgment.[10]

The second action of grace in "Revelation" comes with the message that God speaks to Mrs. Turpin. After hosing down the "pig parlor," Ruby rails against God like the prophets of old in her earnest rage to understand. "'Go on,' she yelled, 'call me a hog! Call me a hog again. From hell. Call me a wart hog from hell. Put that bottom rail on top. There'll still be a top and bottom!'" Here we learn that Ruby is well aware of the teaching that "the last shall be first." If you put the bottom rail on top, there will always be a top and a bottom! Very true, quite reasonable. But again she fails to grasp the tremendous *mercy* of God, preferring the sensible-seeming prudence of human justice. At last, and in a final surge of ferocity, she roars, "'Who do you think you are?' . . . the question carried over the pasture and across the highway and the cotton field and returned to her clearly like an answer from beyond the wood." ("Revelation," *CW,* 653)

---

10. James 2:1-13.

In her own echoing voice, God answers Ruby: Who do you think *you* are? It is the same answer God gave Job: "Where were you when I founded the earth?"[11]

> Then like a monumental statue coming to life, she bent her head slowly and gazed, as if through the very heart of mystery, down into the pig parlor at the hogs . . . they seemed to pant with a secret life . . . At last she lifted her head. . . . ("Revelation," *CW*, 653)

Now O'Connor delivers the third action of grace, depicting the tremendous revelation that God grants to this prideful, demanding, reasonable-seeming but wrong, good woman:

> A visionary light settled in her eyes. She saw . . . a vast horde of souls were rumbling toward heaven. There were whole companies of white-trash, clean for the first time in their lives, and bands of black niggers in white robes, and battalions of freaks and lunatics shouting and clapping and leaping like frogs. And bringing up the end of the procession was a tribe of people whom she recognized at once as those who, like herself and Claud, had always had a little of everything and the God-given wit to use it right. She leaned forward to observe them closer. They were marching behind the others with great dignity, accountable as they had always been for good order and common sense and respectable behavior. They alone were on key. Yet she could see by their shocked and altered faces that even their virtues were being burned away. ("Revelation," *CW*, 653-54)

Even their *virtues* were being burned away! Ruby *is* virtuous. She is grateful to God for Claud and for her own life, for being what she is and having what she has. She is *virtuous*. Yet humility is the foundation of all virtues. O'Connor is showing that any virtue, without humility, is like carrying straw against the wind. Without humility, there is the real danger that our good works will become a source of pride, which is deadly. And what is Ruby Turpin's great sin but pride? In order to be a fit recipient of grace, she will need to

11. Job 38:4.

take a hard look at those panting pigs. "God resists the proud, but gives grace to the humble," St. James warns us.[12] John Garvey, you may recall, made a similar point: "The people who are the most open to grace are those who know how broken they are."[13]

While humility prepares us for grace, it does exact its price. For Mrs. Turpin, it takes a literal crack in the head and an exhortation by some mysterious force to get her to see herself as humble as a hog. But Ruby's direction has been altered and, like O. E. Parker, she is now on her proper path home.

> At length she got down and turned off the faucet and made her slow way on the darkening path to the house. In the woods around her the invisible cricket choruses had struck up, but what she heard were the voices of the souls climbing upward into the starry field and shouting hallelujah. ("Revelation," *CW*, 654)

In these two stories we learn that redemption itself comes at a cost. Ruby must pay the price for her humble new beginning. O. E. Parker, with Christ embedded in his flesh, will also pay a price. "That'll cost you plenty," warns the tattoo artist, remember? Writes O'Connor: "There is something in us, as story-tellers and as listeners to stories, that demands the redemptive act, that demands that what falls at least be offered the chance to be restored. The reader of today looks for this motion, and rightly so, but what he has forgotten is the cost of it."[14]

What is the cost of redemption? After sin and repentance, what else is required of us? Jean-Baptiste knew, and recoiled. It is a price that our next likable hero will understand and pay, however reluctantly.

12. James 4:6.

13. Garvey, "Something is Wrong: That's the Beginning of Wisdom," 8.

14. O'Connor, "Some Aspects of the Grotesque in Southern Fiction," *CW*, 820.

8. The Vocation of Love in Graham Greene's *The Power and the Glory*

Graham Greene

Biographic Notes

GRAHAM GREENE WAS BORN in England in 1904, and died in 1991. He was a convert to Catholicism, but only for the practical purpose of marrying a Catholic girl. He had a very difficult childhood and was tormented in school. Struggling as an adolescent with depression, he ran away and even attempted suicide on more than one occasion as a teen. His father sent him to psychoanalysis where he spent six months living with his analyst. He claimed that these were the happiest days of his life.

Because his conversion to Catholicism at the age of twenty-two was not a spiritual conversion, he had no emotional commitment to the faith. He did affirm the logic of it—though not without doubt—and in fact, chose the name Thomas the Doubter as his baptismal name. He did not doubt the church or the teachings of Jesus; what he doubted was the existence of God. He could never fully accept the reality of God's existence and called himself a Catholic atheist; perhaps with tongue in cheek, but perhaps not!

The theme throughout Greene's writing is the action of grace within the context of sin. Though moments of grace are rare in his novels, when it does appear it is "like a vertical shaft of hope to exorcise the simmering despair."[1] Like O'Connor, Greene readily knew that sin and violence can prepare one for the onset of grace, even in the devil's own territory, and sometimes because of it. For Greene, this territory was the human heart.

Graham Greene was himself a sinful man. He was an unfaithful husband, taking mistresses along with him as he traveled, extensively and publically. He said he went to Mexico to avoid a Hollywood lawsuit brought on by a rather insinuating review he wrote regarding Shirley Temple's coquettish appeal to "old men and clergymen." And while he stated, again and again, that he hated the place, it was from his travels in Mexico (toting along a mistress, doubting his faith, running from a lawsuit, and despising the hosts of the land he moved through) that he was able to write this masterpiece of martyrdom, *The Power and the Glory*.

A Brief Overview of the Mexican Revolution

Because we North Americans know so little about our North American neighbors to the south (even the fact that Mexico *is* a North American country), I want to give a brief contextual history of that country in the twentieth century, as it pertains to the Mexican revolution and the Catholic Church in general, and to Greene's *The Power and the Glory* in particular.

After centuries of Spanish rule, and by the middle of the nineteenth century, Mexico was a country owned almost entirely by a few wealthy families. These grand lords held massive, nation-sized estates, while the oppressed peasantry struggled to survive.

The revolution of 1910 removed President Porfirio Dias Mori from power and ended his decades-long dictatorship. A Constitutional Republic was established in its place. But when the 1917 constitution was confirmed, it was clearly anticlerical. The church was charged with being anti-science, too conservative, too closely knit to the old oligarchy and to European powers. The

1. Pearce, "Graham Greene, Doubter Par Excellence."

revolutionary Mexican state sought to eliminate the influence of the Catholic Church, not because the church was counter-revolutionary, but because the social teachings of the church rivaled the post-revolutionary party. This tension was not so much an ideological conflict of revolutionaries vs. reactionaries as it was a power struggle between rivals for the hearts of the people.

In 1926 the people revolted against the post-revolutionary government. They rebelled against the city elite, the northerners, and the wealthy. These "Cristeros," as they were called, were devout Catholics and opposed the anti-church government which threatened them.

The Vatican called for peace. Pope Pius XI wrote three encyclicals on the state of affairs in Mexico and requested that the Mexican hierarchy work to persuade the Cristeros to lay down their arms in order to reach an agreement with the government. Under pressure from the United States a compromise was reached in 1929 and the Cristeros put down their weapons. The compromise, however, allowed the Mexican elite to maintain control over the government and betray the unarmed Cristeros. Five-hundred of their leaders were rounded up and shot, along with five-thousand of their men, and then their family properties were seized.

The obedience of the Cristeros to the Holy See, and the betrayal of the revolutionary government against the Cristeros, was a disaster to Mexican Catholicism. By 1930, direct reprisals against the Catholic clergy began. The church now fell under the control of the state and under the rule of Pluterco Elias Calles. His law closed the churches and schools, outlawed the Mass, and forced priests to either marry (be laicized) or be executed. Most fled to safer states, but many were shot by firing squads, crying "*Viva el Cristo Rey!*" with their arms outstretched in the form of the cross.

By 1940, the church in Mexico had no tangible existence, no property, no schools, no monasteries or convents, no foreign priests, no right to defend itself in court, and no lawful authorization to celebrate Mass. Some forty priests were killed or executed, 2,500 went into hiding, and many, including the Mexican bishops, were exiled. In 1926 there were 3,000 priests practicing their faith for fifteen million people. By 1934 there were only 334 priests allowed to minister to the same fifteen million.[2]

Graham Greene traveled to Mexico in 1937 and 1938, when the greater persecutions against the church were waning. Still, he was horrified by the government's mistreatment of the church, and would later use the tragic landscape of Mexico (and the southern states where the persecutions were most horrific) for his novel, *The Power and the Glory.* He did not travel to Mexico to find some exotic background for a new novel. He was intending to dodge the Hollywood lawsuit and to study the political situation there. On his journeys, however, he met character after character, each worthy and odd enough to people a future work that would be set within this strange, "huge abandonment" of a country.

The war claimed the lives of some 90,000 people: 56,882 on the federal side and 30,000 Cristeros. There were also many civilians and Cristeros killed in anti-clerical raids well after the war had ended. For decades, the Calles laws remained on the books, though few attempts were made by the *federales* to enforce them. Nevertheless, in several localities, officials continued to persecute Catholic priests based on their own interpretations of the law.

The Mexican government finally amended its Constitution by granting all religious groups legal status, conceding them limited property rights, and lifting restrictions on the number of priests allowed to practice their faith; all this taking place in *1992.*

Vocation and Holy Orders

The Power and the Glory is a novel about vocation. In particular, it is about the vocation of the ordained priesthood, but it is not without its own sideways look at the vocation of marriage (the other sacrament of vocation), as broken, brief, and discouraging as this look seems to be. Neither the priests nor the few fractured couples are exemplary people. Their dignity, when it is found—and it takes

---

2. Van Hove, SJ, Review of *Blood Drenched Altars*, 3.

some work to find it—is in their fidelity to their calling, not in their own personal goodness.

How is this calling defined for us in Catholic theology? According to the Catechism, the ordained priesthood, or holy orders, "is the sacrament through which the mission entrusted by Christ to his apostles continues to be exercised in the Church until the end of time . . . "[3]

We are each called to be the person that God created us to be. We are to live our lives in freedom and dignity and to realize our gifts and God-given potential. As Christians, we are on a mission to bear witness to the truth of Christ and the gospels. Because we are bearers of the incarnate Christ and inheritors of Christ's dignity, we are not only sanctified by the Incarnation, but are baptized into the death of Christ. That is, we are called into union with God through love and self-sacrifice.

The two sacraments of vocation, holy orders and holy matrimony, are directed primarily toward the salvation of others. The Catechism states: "If (matrimony and holy orders) contribute as well to personal salvation, it is through the service to others that they do so."[4] For the married couple, it is through their love for one another and their love for the children they bring into the world. Their role is to be Christ to one another, as spouses and as a family. For the ordained priest, it is through his priestly ministry to Christ's Bride, the church. What is unique and particular about the ordained priesthood, according to Thomas Merton, is that the priest is called to "keep alive in the world the *sacramental presence and action* of the Risen Savior."[5] The priest acts in the person of Jesus Christ. The priest is "a visible human instrument" of Christ who "sanctifies and governs the Church."[6] He not only gives his life to the church, *he gives his body* over to the church in a unique way. As the married pair give their bodies to one another in a sacramental union, safeguarded by their vows, the priest gives his

3. *Catechism of the Catholic Church*, 1536.
4. Ibid., 1534.
5. Merton, *No Man is an Island*, 146. Emphasis mine.
6. Ibid., 146.

body to the church, safeguarded by his vows of celibacy and obedience, and through his sacramental ministry. "For, to speak plainly," Merton tells us, "the priest makes no sense at all in the world except to perpetuate in it the sacrifice of the Cross, and to die with Christ on the Cross for the love of those whom God would have him save."[7]

The Power and the Glory

The Power and the Glory is fractured into many mini-stories, like a kaleidoscope, with each segment presented through a particular point of view and by various minor and major players. The heart of the tale centers upon the "whisky priest," a fugitive running from the authorities in a state where Catholicism is outlawed.[8] All of these characters and their small stories build and layer upon one another to give the reader a multi-angled look at post-revolution Mexico, the church, the Mexican people, and their heroes.

The first chapter begins with the lonely actions of an aging English dentist, Mr. Trench, as he goes about his business at some unnamed southern port. He strikes up a casual conversation with the priest-protagonist because the shabby man speaks excellent English, but the priest might just as well have been any insignificant "stranger" in the background of the story. Thinking that this stranger might have a bottle of brandy on him (in a state where liquor is outlawed), Mr. Trench invites him to his office and they share a drink together. (Mr. Trench bears a strong resemblance to Graham Greene!) Soon a young boy comes to the dentist's dwelling looking for a "doctor." He says his mother is dying and a "doctor" is needed. The unnamed stranger gets up, reluctantly, and climbs onto the boy's mule to be led away into the swampy interior, thus missing the boat that would otherwise have taken him to safety and freedom.

7. Ibid., 147.
8. The state is not identified, though it is likely Tabasco or Chiapas.

It is significant that the story begins this peculiar way, from the perspective of Mr. Trench, whose observations are treated as if he were the key character (when in fact, he is minor) and where the hero (a Mexican, and yet a "stranger") is pushed far to the background. The significance will be demonstrated for us again in the novel's last chapter, as the story ends in the same manner, with Mr. Trench in his dental office gazing at a scene some distance away. Everything that Graham Greene detested about Mexico seems to live under a microscope in *The Power and the Glory*. The place is hot, unbearably hot. There is sickness, mud, disease, jungles, superstition, loneliness, and tremendous poverty. On top of all that, it is a world infested with vermin; insects, exploding beetles, mosquitoes, parasites, flies, vultures, and fleas, all feeding on the flesh of a feverish people, on their quivering beasts, countless rats, and the murdered bodies of their neighbors. It is no place for heroes.

As we move into the interior of the state, we are introduced to the families who live in the small farming villages. In particular we meet an anonymous family consisting of two pious girls, a devout mother, a practical father, and a restless teenage son. They once sheltered the "whisky priest" to save his life, but the mother is scandalized by his drunken ways. "He smelled funny," the little girls say. At a baptism in the village he was so drunk that he baptized a baby boy, who should have been christened "Pedro," with the girl's name "Carlota." Now that boy must carry his baptismal name, Carlota, around with him for the rest of his life! One can smile at the humor, but there is a serious matter to consider here as well. "Carlota" will be entered into the parish registers, which is tragic enough, but remember that our baptismal name is of great significance, as we have seen in previous stories and certainly according to the teachings of the church. This is the name by which we are known to God. The mother understands the scandal, and in this family it is the mother who is most diligent about her church and faith.

This mother reads stories of the saints and martyrs to her children for the sake of their education in the faith, and is therefore fulfilling her vocation as a mother and as an instrument of her children's salvation. The saintly stories are candy-coated for children, and the two little girls gobble them up. The fourteen year old boy, however, is no longer impressed by the pretty, even sissified tales of piety. He prefers stories of adventure. When the police come through his village, all the boys gawk in awe at their weaponry. The soldiers are a tremendous sight, handsomely dressed, and not like the children's farmer fathers. The pistol that the noble lieutenant wears is an impressive symbol of power. Can they touch it? This is the state's clarion call to its young peasants. If these boys want to escape a dreary life of poverty and back-breaking work, if they want to be significant, wear sharp uniforms and lead a life of adventure, then they should join the armed forces and become the very instruments of a state that will keep their families oppressed. Many join up.

As for the noble lieutenant, he does not believe that he is an instrument of oppression; that was in a different age. He believes he is a hero of liberation. He is the future: an idealistic and dedicated young soldier, virtuous and patriotic. The lieutenant truly cares about the welfare of his countrymen. He loves the people, and his love is real. He wants to give his life to improve their lives in the world. He is a communist, an atheist, a secular saint, and in the end a success, because he does get his man. He captures the last priest in the state, someone he believes is a swindler—like the priests he knew when he was a child—a charlatan who bewitches the people with superstition and fear. But the reader's sympathies are not likely with the lieutenant. When the soldier finally meets the "whisky priest" after his capture, and when they have time to sit down and talk, the lieutenant undergoes a change of heart. He is moved to grant the priest his last request and makes a dangerous visit to Padre José, asking him to meet with the "whisky priest" to hear his confession. To the lieutenant's credit, this merciful act may well lead to his own salvation.

In Padre José, however, we haven't much to admire, only pity. Here is a priest who has acquiesced to the state; a sad, fat, and impotent married-man. He is mocked by the town's children and nagged by his former house-keeper, now his wife. He is miserable in his marriage, like O. E. Parker, but he can find no easy way out. Padre José did not marry for love, he married to save his neck. Under the country's cruel regime, it was either marry or be shot, and he made the obvious choice, but he is thoroughly ashamed of himself. The children of the village taunt him with his own name. They mimic the voice of his wife and call out from the bushes: "José! Come to bed José!" But the children don't anger him. He knows they are right. He knows that he is a buffoon. "An old man who married was grotesque enough, but an old priest. . . . He stood outside himself and wondered whether he was even fit for hell." (*TPTG*, 29)

But self-knowledge does not lead Padre José to do the hard work that could change him. Time and time again opportunities are presented where he might still do the heroic thing—to hide the "whisky priest" and save his life, or hear his last confession and save his soul—but Padre José cringes and refuses these opportunities. It's true that his wife won't allow it, but it's just as true that José is a coward. Rather than defy her illicit claim on him (he is stymied by his two conflicting vows of obedience), José avoids the conflict entirely. He does not follow the way of duty, or loyalty, or happiness, or even the way of the flesh. Instead he takes the easiest way possible, and that is his undoing. It is so contrary to the way of the cross! This is also why, as he well knows, "the whole world was blanketed with his own sin." (*TPTG*, 29) Like Jean-Baptiste, he can hear the universe laughing at him. While he was once a highly respected cleric, he is now just a joke. " . . . the lieutenant laughed once—a poor unconvincing addition to the general laughter which now surrounded Padre José, ringing up all round to the disciplined constellations he had once known by name." (*TPTG*, 244)

Let us turn now to the "whisky priest," our hero, such as he is. We do not know his name, as it is never given in the story (notice that Padre José *is* named, however). One must wonder why the "whisky priest" is not given a name, just this derogatory title. It is surely not because his name is unimportant, nor is it an oversight by the author. Our hero is presented as a man remote and a little absurd. He is certainly a weakling, a drunkard, and on the run. Out of loneliness and desire he has fathered a child that he cannot properly support. He giggles, he complains, he sets a bad example for the village children, and he even drinks the wine he was to use for Mass. As the village father says to his wife (in the little anonymous family introduced earlier), they have been abandoned and such is their church: a drunkard for a priest and Padre José, the town joke. Their only other choice, if they don't like it, is to leave the church. "I would rather die," the mother retorts.

The "whisky priest" is on a journey, sometimes directed towards freedom across the state border, sometimes directed back to minister to a soul in need, but he does not walk alone. He has a companion. The half-caste is a strange accompaniment. He comes and goes and reappears whenever it seems to suit him. His front teeth are missing, so he has only two canine "fangs" that show through his lips. This is no subtle clue! The half-caste is the voice and presence of the devil. This devil knows where the priest is wounded and festers there like an infection. The half-caste hounds the priest, begging for his pity. He will be the "whisky priest's" betrayer, but he sees himself only as a victim. His pronouncements are always self-serving. It is a pity that no one trusts him. His life is so tragic, he moans, how can he help himself? He repeats over and over again that he is a Christian, a good Catholic, but the priest does not minister to him. Somehow the priest knows who the mestizo is, and what he is about to do. "He was in the presence of Judas." (*TPTG*, 106) And when our hero finds the half-caste shivering from fever, he wonders—charitably—if he is mistaken. But then he looks up and sees "the yellow malarial eyes of the mestizo watching him." The priest thinks to himself: "Christ would not have found Judas sleeping in the garden: Judas could watch more than one hour." (*TPTG*, 107)

This little cat and mouse game between the "whisky priest" and the half-caste is necessary to the story and the theology. Even though the reader well knows that this Judas is plotting to turn the priest in for the bounty money, somehow it has to be. St. Luke tells us that the devil entered Judas, and so he betrayed Christ. The great action of grace in this novel requires the territory of the devil. Indeed, it seems to require the devil himself. Like Jean-Baptiste, the "whisky priest" is acutely aware of his own sinfulness, but there is tremendous love in him, too. Like Hazel Motes, the "whisky priest" is running from Christ and the cross, but intuitively he knows that it is his fate. He is also like Ruby Turpin, proud (as the young priest depicted in the photo), but learning, too, the hard virtue of humility. He tells himself that he did not flee the persecutions when he had the chance because of his daughter, Brigida, whom he loves. Yet he does not believe his own justifications. He knows better. No, he did not remain in the state for the sake of his child, whom he barely knows and cannot support, and who seems to be destined for some tragic end. Neither did he stay because of his priestly ministry. He concludes that it was his pride that kept him working in the treacherous state, when all the other priests and bishops had fled north. He remained because he thought he could endure what the others could not. Now he is ashamed of his earlier pride. In the end, of course, his actions are heroic, though he likely never knew it to be the case.

He is a reluctant priest and a reluctant martyr, it's true; yet he somehow manages to administer nearly all of the sacraments of the church. He hears the confessions of the people, celebrates secret Masses, baptizes their children, buries the dead, anoints the sick, marries the cohabitating couples, and travels vast distances— at great risk—to fulfill his priestly duties. When the police begin to take hostages, killing those who refuse to betray the priest's whereabouts, he is shouldered with an even greater burden. Now, the people are dying for him! They are taking his place, and the place of Christ on the cross, so that he can continue to live and serve them as their unworthy priest. He wants comfort, he wants freedom, yet he knows that he is called to something greater, and always he returns to the call of his people. If the vocation of the priest is to perpetuate the sacrifice of the cross in the world—through the sacraments of the church which he performs, and through the real sacrifice of his own flesh—then the "whisky priest," as weak as he is, fulfills this vocation with stunning beauty.

We have learned to look for the action of grace in sacramental literature. Where is the action of grace in this novel? It is not as clearly stated as one might find in a story by Flannery O'Connor, for example, but the moments do exist. Perhaps there is no event more meaningful than his experience in the prison, after he is arrested and thrown into a dark dungeon with scores of other unfortunate souls. It is here that our hero discovers, perhaps for the first time in his life, that he really loves all of these people. Even in their sinfulness, their vulgarities and their treachery, he loves them. When he sees his smug photograph in the lieutenant's office, he wonders if it is possible that our venial sins are the sins that cut us off from grace. The worst sins can make a person suffer such guilt that grace is readily recognized when it is offered.

> It was for this world that Christ had died; the more evil you saw and heard about you, the greater glory lay around the death. It was too easy to die for what was good or beautiful, for home or children or a civilization—it needed a God to die for the half-hearted and corrupt. (*TPTG*, 114)

Among the many odd characters in this work there is a most out-of-place couple—a brother and sister—who give the "whisky priest" a place to rest from his travels. These are the Lutheran Lehrs, a clean, sterile, non-sexual, German-American pair. They live a respectable life on a fine estate, but they are barren, living without any discernable purpose. Still, they are very kind to the priest. He eats with them, bathes in the creek with Mr. Lehr, sleeps in their home, and holds Mass in their barn for the villagers and the Indians who have walked fifty miles to attend. It seems a strange episode, but there is something vital in these contrasting worlds of the shabby, fugitive priest—who drinks too much brandy and performs illegal acts of worship—and the good Protestant siblings who are restful, well-washed, peaceful, and a little dull. Though they disagree with his church, they shelter the priest and allow him to commit these sacred, criminal acts on their land. They are bold enough to dare, and old enough not to care about the police and their Mexican legalities. The Christian thing to do is give this man-of-the-cloth a place to lay his head as well as food and cloth-ing for his journey. Graciously, he accepts their hospitality. It is an odd respite, but it is an essential contrast. Here are the good and beautiful who do not need a God to die for them.

Once the "whisky priest" leaves the Lehrs he is joined again by the half-caste who leads him away. It is a great relief when the "whisky priest" foils his pursuers and manages to cross the border into safety at last. But his security is short-lived. The mestizo tells him that he is needed by a Yankee bandit, "a good Catholic," who has been shot and is asking for a priest back in their home state. The "whisky priest" cannot refuse him the sacraments and last rites, the man is dying. So, wearily, our hero crosses back over the border, knowing full well that this is a trap and he will be captured. Even the reader knows that the half-caste will succeed with his plan and earn his bounty.

The priest finds the uncooperative gringo and gives him a conditional absolution before he dies. Immediately following, the lieutenant appears to arrest him.

The dutiful lieutenant will take the priest all the way across the state for trial and a sure execution, but the "whisky priest" is ready. He has had enough of running. This final journey will al-low the priest time to spend with the good lieutenant, to discuss their differences and to move (just a little) the soldier's heart. He explains to the lieutenant the differences between their two voca-tions. "It's no good your working for your end unless you're a good man yourself. And there won't always be good men in your party. Then you'll have all the old starvation, beating, get-rich-anyhow. But it doesn't matter so much my being a coward—and all the rest. I can put God into a man's mouth just the same—and I can give him God's pardon. It wouldn't make any difference to that if every priest in the Church was like me." (*TPTG*, 232)

The change is slight, but the lieutenant will defy the law he cherishes and represents in order to retrieve Padre José so he might hear the condemned priest's last confession. This noble ac-tion allows the reader some hope for the good lieutenant. But as we know, Padre José is held back by his wife, submitting to her counterfeit authority, and declines to go. Like Jean-Baptiste (and even when assured safe-passage), he can barely bear to look at the cross, much less shoulder it. Everything, now, is in disorder; all is inverted, confused, and unsettled.

Back in the port town where the story began, we must finally witness the execution of our hero. The event is described from the dentist's office and once again through the eyes of Mr. Trench, who is amazed and even horrified at the scene he sees from his window. This juxtaposition is necessary. We can no longer be with the priest or his thoughts and worries. He will soon die. And though Padre José would not hear his confession, still, the "whisky priest" will die a martyr's death and attain heaven, his courage aided by a gifted bottle of brandy.

> A horrid fascination kept (Mr. Trench) by the window: this was something he had never seen. . . . A small man came out of a side door: he was held up by two policemen, but you could tell that he was doing his best—it was only that his legs were not fully under his control. . . . They paddled him across to the opposite wall: an officer tied a handkerchief round his eyes. Mr. Trench thought: But I know him. Good God, one ought to do something. This was like seeing a neighbor shot. . . . Of course there was nothing to do. Everything went very quickly like a routine. The officer stepped aside, the rifles went up, and the little man suddenly made jerky movements with his arms. He was trying to say something: what was the phrase they were always supposed to use? That was routine too, but perhaps his mouth was too dry, because nothing came out except a word that sounded more like "Excuse." The crash of rifles shook Mr. Trench: they seemed to vibrate inside his own guts: he felt rather sick and shut his eyes. Then there was a single shot, and opening his eyes again he saw the officer stuffing his gun back into his holster, and the little man was a routine heap beside the wall . . . " (*TPTG*, 260-62)

The priest is not saved by his goodness; he is saved through his priestly ministry—which is his vocation—and in his martyrdom. Imperfect as he is, the sacraments themselves, through Christ whom he represents, give grace. And he has administered them to perfection because he has died on account of that ministry.

When the priest was in the prison and reflecting on his execution, he came to a final realization. That judgment was this: How easy it might have been to be a saint. Is the "whisky priest" a saint? Yes, of course, but then why does Greene present his martyrdom with such small regard, as a "little man" drunk on brandy, staggering to his execution? He is so wobbly that he needs to be carried in by the guards. Where is his courage, his faith, his beatific smile? Where is the pageantry? How different this scene is from the stories of the saints that the good mother reads to her children! Or is it possible that our saints are just like any one of us, human, flawed, terrified, and unworthy?

There is still the teenage boy, the young man who once scoffed at the pious stories his mother told, who wanted adventure, who asked to touch the policeman's pistol, and who now feels abandoned. His thoughts go back to the "whisky priest."

> It brought it home to one—to have had a hero in the house, though it had only been for twenty-four hours. And he was the last. There were no more priests and no more heroes. He listened resentfully to the sound of booted feet coming up the pavement. Ordinary life pressed round him. He got down from the window-seat and picked up his candle—Zapata, Villa, Madero, and the rest, they were all dead, and it was people like the man out there who killed them. He felt deceived. (*TPTG*, 265)

When the lieutenant touches his gun and smiles his greeting to the boy, the young man "crinkled up his face and spat through the window bars, accurately, so that a little blob of spittle lay on the revolver-butt." The boy goes to bed, dejected, but then there is a knock at the door. He goes to see.

> A stranger stood in the street: a tall pale thin man with a rather sour mouth, who carried a small suitcase. . . . The stranger said: "I have only just landed. I came up the river tonight. I thought perhaps . . . I have an introduction for the Señora from a great friend of hers."

"She is asleep," the boy repeated.

"If you would let me come in," the man said with an odd frightened smile, and suddenly lowering his voice he said to the boy: "I am a priest."

"You?" the boy exclaimed.

"Yes," he said gently, "My name is Father—" But the boy had already swung the door open and put his lips to his hand before the other could give himself a name. (*TPTG*, 267)

Why is this new priest unnamed? Because his name is *Christ to the world*. That is his vocation and the sacramental gift of holy orders. Now we can see the power and the glory of the "whisky priest's" martyrdom. He is a human being, after all, and not a holy card. He is like us in every way *including* sin. His human life and human death will be added to the calendar of saints, and to this abandoned land's trove of anonymous heroes.

What is the cost of redemption? *The cross, the cross, the cross, the cross.*

What is *your name*? Can you speak it? Will you? You were purchased at a great price.

9. The Point of Suffering in Annie Dillard's *Holy the Firm*

EACH DAY NEW SAINTS and martyrs enter heaven. This is the living, breathing church. When we consider the mother reading to her children in Graham Greene's novel, and the travels of the "whisky priest" who was such a scandal in his life but a true hero in his ministry, we should recollect the importance of stories and recall the words of Fr. Greeley:

> Catholic stories . . . speak of a community of the followers of Jesus bonding with one another to pass on the heritage which is formed by the stories. The doctrines are latent in the stories. Both are necessary, but the stories come first. . . . We worship the God we encounter in the stories.[1]

Even in the sacraments, even in the Mass, we are reliving a story that is centered on an event. The Mass retells the last supper of Jesus before he was crucified on the cross. We are redeemed by this bloody event in our human history, and the Mass reminds us—retelling us again and again—that the cost of redemption is the cross. "This is my body, which will be given up for you."

---

1. Greeley, "Why I'm Still A Catholic."

No Man is an Island

The word of the cross is foolishness to them that perish.
But to them that are saved it is the power of God.

1 Cor 1:18

Thomas Merton's *No Man is an Island* gives us many insights into the sacramental character of our faith. His chapter entitled "The Word of the Cross" takes us into the arduous realm of human suffering. He does not bother with the mundane ruminations on human suffering: that we are being punished for bad behavior. Gerard Manley Hopkins would challenge this, asking "Why do sinners' ways prosper? and why must Disappointment all I endeavour end?"[2] This is a challenge also voiced by Job! Nor does Merton accept the secular notion that there is suffering because that's just the way things are, which is certainly no way for people of faith to be thinking. And he would not accept Nietzsche's grim pronouncement, that "what doesn't kill me only makes me stronger." Hasn't the world seen enough of embittered strong-men? No, Merton rejects these explanations as insufficient and even cruel. "Suffering without faith is a curse,"[3] he tells us, and this is a curse that Jean-Baptiste knew personally: "Ah, *mon cher*, for anyone who is alone, without God and without a master, the weight of days is dreadful." (*The Fall*, 133)

Counter to these ineffectual attempts at explaining suffering on human terms, Merton takes us into the *mystery* of suffering by taking us to the foot of the cross. He reminds us that we have been baptized into the death of Christ. Suffering, then, is bound up in our baptismal identity, where we find our vocation in our conformity to the life of Christ and in his suffering. "For baptism is the application to our souls of the Passion of Christ."[4] We are called, then, not only to accept suffering but to "make it holy."

2. See Gerard Manley Hopkins' poem: "Thou art indeed just Lord, if I contend With thee; but sir, so what I plead is just."
3. Merton, *No Man is an Island*, 96.
4. Ibid., 95.

What actions or works in the literature we have reviewed touch upon this mystery? Who among our protagonists sets out to make suffering holy?

In his own way, Hazel Motes imposes suffering and bodily mortifications upon himself as an act of penance; Jean-Baptiste, who knew what was required of him, could only accept and preach the idea of it, but not the final, chilly action; and more perfectly the "whisky priest," who obeys his calling whenever someone is in need of a priest, performing his priestly duties even unto death. "The saint is one so attuned to the spirit and heart of Christ that he is compelled to answer the demands of love by a love that matches that of Christ."[5]

Suffering poses the question: "Who are you?" We must answer distinctly, and give our own name; who we are and who we are destined to be, the name by which God knows us.

> Baptism . . . gives us our personal, incommunicable, vocation to reproduce in our own lives the life and sufferings and charity of Christ in a way unknown to anyone else who has ever lived under the sun.[6]

To know this is to know the cross, and to know the cross is to know that we are saved by the suffering of Christ.

> When I see my trials . . . as the sacramental gift of Christ's love, given to me by God the Father along with my identity and my very name . . . then I realize that my suffering is . . . the Passion of Christ, stretching out its tendrils into my life . . . making my soul dizzy with the wine of Christ's love, and pouring that wine as strong as fire upon the whole world.[7]

5. Ibid., 93.
6. Ibid., 95.
7. Ibid., 96.

Holy the Firm

"Into this world falls a plane."

Annie Dillard's *Holy the Firm* became a book about suffering. It did not start out that way. Dillard set out to spend three days on an island in Puget Sound and to journal about her experiences there. "Teach me thy ways, O Lord," she sang, venturing out on what she expected to be a peaceful, spiritual retreat. She didn't expect much to happen. She didn't expect a plane to fall, neatly, and in her lap so to speak. She says "'Teach me thy ways, O Lord' is, like all prayers, a rash one." (*HTF*, 19) Equally rash was God's response, given to her on the second day of her retreat. She was to write about suffering. It was preordained.

Like *The Fall*, *Holy the Firm* is a brief book, one that should be read two or three times, and the last time backwards. It is also a recollection, a memoir, awash with images and an alterable plot, where time is out of joint and memories out of sequence and stacked. Dillard went on this spiritual journey to study—in awe of creation, even her own—and to pray. She studies the material world around her, mountains, islands, and some of its creatures. She prays to a god/God she can barely name.

"All day long I feel created," she tells us. The Armenians salt their newborn babies; Israel's covenant with God is 'a covenant of salt forever.' "In the Roman church baptism, the priest places salt in the infant's mouth . . . I salt my breakfast eggs." (*HTF*, 25) Here on this island are created sheep, created gulls, and created Annie, who greets her "created meal, amazed." This amazement at being alive, being created, being contingent upon a Creator that we know so little about, grounds us in the material salt-of-the-earth, literally and hard-fast. It grounds the sheep, too, "set down here precisely, just touching their blue shadows hoof to hoof on the grass." It grounds us in the flesh of our bodies. As Jean-Baptiste tells us in his boasting: "I was born to have a body." Isn't it amazing that we are here at all; that there is a "here" even to be in; when really there ought not to have been anything at all? This is Dillard's astonishment, and it is a good one.

In her created world she tells us (quoting Emerson) that "every day is a god." As if divinity existed in the passing of time; as if that divinity can even be guessed at. We should recall the line from Shakespeare's *King Lear*: "As flies to wanton boys are we to the *gods. They kill us for their sport.*" If every day is a god then today is a dangerous god, a god who might kill us at any minute. We are created but we are mortal, too, and time is taking its toll.

She recollects another time; a time when she was reading in the woods by candlelight and a moth flew into the flame. It stuck in the wax of the candle, fried, and then wicked like a "hollow saint, like a flame-faced virgin gone to God." "The wax rose in the moth's body from her soaking abdomen to her thorax to the jabbed hole where her head should be, and widened into flame, a saffron-yellow flame that robed her to the ground like any immolating monk. That candle had two wicks, two flames of identical height, side by side." (*HTF*, 17)

In her cabin on the island, Dillard now directs her gaze outward (from a room like a skull), away from the mineral hard mountains to the blue horizon, to the lines of infinite space where "the corner of infinity clips time." (*HTF*, 24) From there one can almost catch a glimpse of our Creator God, where the corner of Holy meets our ragged edge.

> Into this world falls a plane. The earth is a mineral speckle planted in trees. The plane snagged its wing on a tree, fluttered in a tiny arc, and struggled down. I heard it go. (*HTF*, 35)

> Moths kept flying into the candle . . . they would singe their wings and fall, and their hot wings, as if melted, would stick to the first thing they touched . . . snagged moths could flutter only in tiny arcs. (*HTF*, 15)

> It fell easily; one wing snagged on a fir top; the metal fell down . . . the fuel exploded; and Julie Norwich seven years old burnt off her face. (*HTF*, 36)

Julie Norwich,[8] whose suffering is more severe than any we would want to look at, who is just a child unable to comprehend it, will be Annie Dillard's spiritual subject. She didn't ask for it, I'm sure she didn't want it, but there it is.

Dostoyevsky challenged the religious world in the nineteenth century with his character, Ivan Karamazov, who boldly refused to accept a God who allows children to suffer. But Dillard does not reject God. She sets out, somehow, to make sense out of the horrific suffering of this child and of the consuming God of love she encounters. But such a venture is nonsensical. Sense doesn't have the tools. Rational structures can build tremendous cathedrals of the mind, buttressed, hollow, magnificent, but they all come tumbling down like a house of cards when clipped. Dillard's own experiences, her own keen mind and her dearest deep-down vision and love of beauty and art and mischievous children now lie in piles around her like a collapsed cathedral of cards. What is she supposed to do with all of these holy icons?

To try and make sense out of *Holy the Firm* is to approach it wrongly. Like *The Fall*, it is best to sit with it a while.

Annie Dillard's response to the collapse around her is to shuffle the deck, rearrange the images, and splay them out in some new order. She admits, I think, that this is all she can do. "What can an artist use but materials, such as they are? . . . What can an artist set on fire but his world?" (*HTF,* 72) Her tools are words, her subject is suffering, and her skill is honed by study and an unwavering eye. She can only go as far as her gift allows, but her gift is God's life within her. How far will she go?

Instead of theory or discourse, Dillard gives us image after image, linked images and repeated images, until our minds are dizzy with disorder. You might recall *The Litany of Loreto*, that beautiful series of supplications to our Blessed Mother who, in a similar way, is inundated with images and similes: Vessel of honor, Ark of the covenant, Tower of ivory, Mystical rose, Gate of heaven,

8. "Julie Norwich" is a pseudonym, a name contrived from 'Julian of Norwich,' a fourteenth century Catholic mystic. Dillard wrote of Julian of Norwich often in her other works, most notably in *Pilgrim at Tinker Creek.*

Seat of Wisdom, Morning star. This is *sacramental language.* You might recall "Hagia Sophia," where Merton writes:

> She is in all things like the air receiving the sunlight. In her they prosper. In her they glorify God. In her they rejoice to reflect Him. In her they are united with him. She is the union between them. She is the Love that unites them. She is life as communion, life as thanksgiving, life as praise, life as festival, life as glory. ("Hagia Sophia," 66-67)

Merton cannot identify Sophia, she is beyond naming; she is mystery and can only be *likened* to something already known. Dillard—who woke weak to the sound of a plane crash and not strong to the voice of mercy—attempts to do something similar in *Holy the Firm.* For Dillard, suffering is a mystery that cannot be explained, but it can be looked at and experienced and likened to.

What are the most prevalent images Dillard uses in her work? Here are the more notable:

| Moths | Arcs / Arches | Fire | Islands | Faces | Candles | G/gods |
| Time | Clouds | Nuns | Gaps | Salt | Ribs | Wings |

So what happens when we toss these images like cards, how do they fall? How are they linked and suited, colored and numbered, and how does this tangle of icons reconnect, layer and fan out?

Let's consider the many ARCHES:

The moth carcasses consumed by the spider.

The moth's body consumed by flame.

The moth's ribs are a "buttressed vault," shot through with light.

Annie's ribs are full of light, aglow from the communion wine she carries in her backpack.

A cathedral, with its flying buttresses.

The tiny arc of the falling, flaming moth and the falling, flaming plane.

Or, the ISLANDS on Puget Sound:

Appearing and disappearing.

Named and unnamed.

Islands as gods.

Christ baptized, lifting from the water.

Water beads like worlds on his back.

"Water as heavy as planets" and Christ standing on stones.

Worlds that are translucent (beings, things, us) and whole.

Or, the FLAMING FACE (of suffering and adoration):

A moth's head ablaze by fire.

A child's face ablaze by fire.

A saint's face ablaze in prayer.

The seraph's faces ablaze with adoration of God.

An artist's "face is flame like a seraph's."

Israel's chariots of flame.

Dillard ties all of these images together to say, what? Is it apparent? Any serious student of literature would recognize that this is metaphorical language she is using. And if we were to view these metaphors like threads in a tapestry, or the brush strokes of an impressionistic painting, we might know that we need to step away from the strings and dots, lose our focus, and wait for the whole pattern to emerge. Can we do it now? This is the challenge.

At the beginning of our study, in the segment entitled Stories, I posed the question: how is *Holy the Firm* a work of Catholic literature? Yes, it is likely that Dillard wrote it at a time in her life when she was moving closer to the Catholic Church, but that is hardly an explanation. There are plenty of bad writers in RCIA![9]

9. RCIA: Rite of Christian Initiation for Adults; where one attends classes to learn more about the Catholic faith, and perhaps be received into the Catholic Church.

Flannery O'Connor reminds us that our experience of reality and the artist's gesture in depicting that reality (using materials, such as they are) can barely help but discover the divine that imbues it. This artist's action, O'Connor tells us, "would be a gesture which somehow made contact with mystery." Such a revelation is not done easily in the abstract language of theology, but it can be done by skilled artists, according to their gifts. When a poet is good and true and honest, and when the vision before them is real, then their poetic, metaphorical language will—by the grace of God—flower into revelation. It must reveal some aspect of the divine, because the artist is now *in touch with* mystery. Dillard does not take the transcendental route to holiness, she goes into the gaps, the crags, at base, and penetrates created reality (where Hagia Sophia plays before the Creator) only to discover with magnificent insight that 'the firm' arches back into holiness; the Absolute. Holy the Firm.

When we read the closing pages of *Holy the Firm* we are given a very graphic image to contemplate. It is painstakingly structured and intentionally visual. In part it states:

> Esoteric Christianity, I read, posits a substance. It is a created substance, lower than metals and minerals . . . but never on the surface of planets where men could discern it; and it is in touch with the Absolute, at base. . . . The name of this substance is: Holy the Firm. . . .
>
> Scholarship has long distinguished between two strains of thought which proceed in the West from human knowledge of God. In one, the ascetic's metaphysic, the world is far from God. Emanating from God, and linked to him by Christ, the world is yet infinitely other than God. . . . This notion makes, to my mind, a vertical line of the world, a great chain of burning. The more accessible and universal view . . . is scarcely different from pantheism: that the world is immanation, that God is in the thing, and eternally present here, if nowhere else. By these lights the world is flattened on a horizontal plane, singular, all here, crammed with heaven, and alone. But I know that it is not alone, nor singular, nor all. The notion of immanence needs a handle, and the two ideas

themselves need a link, so that life can mean aught to the one, and Christ to the other. (*HTF,* 69-70)

The following graphic attempts to illustrate what these pages are describing. It may not suffice to depict the vision that Dillard is imaging in her language, but some attempt seems necessary. Perhaps you can draw your own.

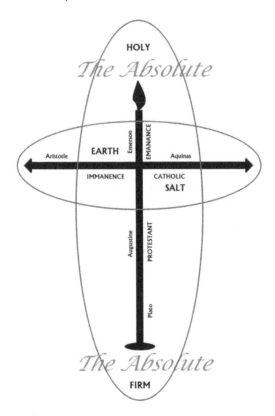

Here, in a unique and graphic way, we can see the parting of the two ancient traditions that splintered Aristotle from Plato,[10] St. Thomas from St. Augustine, and Martin Luther from St. Thomas. Emanance, the ascetic's spiritual reality where God is in His heaven, flames upward, fleeing the gaps and crags of earthly things and shuffling off created flesh in a transcending movement away from matter and chaff; launching (forever launching) into the ideal. Immanence, where God is in the thing, branches outward upon a flat horizon, an experiential plane; spreading away into chaos and whatever. Each tradition is limited by human failings; each meets its handle, its link, its crux, in the center and the cross of Christ.

There are dangers on either path. The vertical can lose touch with earthly salts and become too ethereal and abstract, condemning flesh as evil, at odds with the Eucharist and the Incarnation; what Catholics often accuse Protestants of becoming. Just so, the horizontal, immanent path (the sacramental) can become too rich and sanctify the material to the point of pantheism, paganism, and idolatry; what Protestants often accuse Catholics of becoming. The imaginations differ, but the center holds.

This is Dillard's cruciform, and this is the point.

For Annie Dillard, suffering seems to fracture our sacramental view that the universe mirrors God. Just look closely at the frog in *Pilgrim at Tinker Creek!* If the little frog doesn't stir your sympathies then look at Julie Norwich (if you dare) and ask with Annie Dillard (if you dare): "What in the Sam Hill is going on here?" (*HTF,* 60) She finds a kindred spirit in Origen's view that nature, too, is fallen, but it isn't enough and she knows it. Suffering is the fulcrum of her dilemma where she discovers Christ at the center, and the center holds. The two paths are not a divergence that divides but a convergence that binds and arches back and assumes the whole world and human thought. When the Word became

10. You may recall Raphael's "School of Athens," that famous fresco that decorates the walls of the Apostolic Palace in the Vatican. The focal figures are Plato and Aristotle debating with one another. Plato, the idealist, points skyward, invoking transcendence as the source of true knowledge; while Aristotle, the realist, points earthward, claiming that experience in the world is the path of true knowledge.

Flesh—when God became man, when Emanance touched Immanence—it assumed the universe.[11]

How can we know this? Because we are in touch with, *in touch with*, **in touch with**, all that we experience—embodied—in the world, yet our heads are aflame in praise, our arms outstretched to the horizons, eyes in a skull looking outward, feet paddling us along and doing the best they can: "*Viva el Cristo Rey!*"

We are holy temples all; hollow like a cathedral, arching, lit, and buttressed; peopled inside by water drops and worlds, some hanging on to the altar rail to keep from flying,[12] transcendent. We live in a universe of ideas and matter, of contradictions and paradox. There is suffering and there is Christ on the cross. We are matter and we are spirit. God is spirit, and yet the created, material world is suffused with God, a world that is bloody and eaten and chomped. "*Hoc est corpus meum!*"[13]

In Pilgrim at Tinker Creek, Dillard quotes Ralph Waldo Emerson, that paragon of transcendentalism, in his depiction of a dream:

> I dreamed that I floated at will in the great Ether, and I saw this world floating also not far off, but diminished to the size of an apple. Then an angel took it in his hand and brought it to me and said, "This must thou eat," And I ate the world.[14]

Would that Emerson had believed in the Eucharist!

Dillard continues: "The joke of the world is less like a banana peel than a rake, the old rake in the grass. . . . You wake up with a

---

11. Recollect Hopkins' poem, "The Windhover," where the regal falcon masters the skies; not falling like a singed moth from a candle flame, but swinging forth in ecstasy on a fine arching bow-bend. It is a different image, a different view, but the same conundrum.

12. A reference to St. Teresa of Avila, a sixteenth century mystic, saint and Doctor of the Church who, in her prayerful raptures, was said to have experienced levitations. The other sisters had to hold on to her while she gripped the altar rail to keep from flying away.

13. "This is my body."

14. Dillard, *Pilgrim at Tinker Creek*, 271.

piece of tree in your skull . . . with fruit on our hands . . . a plane falls." (*HTF*, 42)

We are jarred awake, struck in the skull, by suffering. How different this is from Merton's soft awakening in "Hagia Sophia." Yet, these juxtapositions are important! Both are at work in the world, and both are at work in us.

In the final pages of *Holy the Firm* the language settles and Dillard seems to reach a sober resolution: that Julie Norwich will be fixed by surgeons and lead a semi-normal life, and that she (Annie, the artist) "will be the nun for you." Is this resolution (if it is a resolution) satisfying? It is a sacrificial act, but do you buy it? I recall one student's disappointment with the ending. "Did Dillard actually become a nun? Or is this just poetry?" Good question; but why "just?" She certainly became a remarkable writer, with all the work and sacrifice necessary to her craft. Still, one has to wonder if the salvation of the artist, failed or otherwise, can be achieved through their art?[15] We suffer in our art but is it enough? Was confession and penance enough for Jean-Baptiste, who could not accept the grace that was offered him? Dillard claims she will be the nun for the little burnt girl, and Jean-Baptiste's confessor must "sleep on the ground" for him. Each recognizes what is needed; each moves a little shy of the cross. Don't we all? Don't you?

There are some notable similarities between Dillard and Camus in these two significant works, as we have seen. And the pages that close both *The Fall* and *Holy the Firm* are especially poignant. Each ends with a vision of glory, a revelation, as well as a response in faith. In *The Fall* we read:

> Everyone will be saved, eh? . . . Come now, admit that you would be flabbergasted if a chariot came down from heaven to carry me off, or if the snow suddenly caught fire. You don't believe it? Nor do I. But still I must go out. (*The Fall*, 146–47)

---

15. Read Flannery O'Connor's "The Enduring Chill" for her take on the salvation of the artist through his art.

In *Holy the Firm* we read:

> . . . then you kneel, clattering with thoughts, ill, or some
> days erupting, some days holding the altar rail, gripping
> the brass-bolt altar rail, so you won't fly. Do you think I
> don't believe this? You have no idea, none. . . . You cry,
> My father, my father, the chariots of Israel, and the horse-
> men thereof! Held, held fast by love in the world like a
> moth in wax, your life a wick, your head on fire with
> prayer . . . you cry God. (*HTF,* 75-76)

Not only are we treated each time to the chariots of Israel, we
must grapple with the struggling author's own burning question:
"Do you think I don't believe this?" The writers are now directing
themselves to their subjects (Jean-Baptiste's confessor and Dillard's
Julie Norwich) and telling them what they must now next do. And
what is that, oh tender believers? Do you know?

They must each become a saint.

In Thomas Merton's autobiography, *The Seven Storey Mountain*, the recently baptized Merton (a convert in young adulthood)
has a notable conversation with Bob Lax, his best friend.

> . . . Lax suddenly turned around and asked me the
> question.
>
> "What do you want to be, anyway?" . . .
>
> "I don't know; I guess what I want is to be a good Catho-
> lic." . . . Lax did not accept it.
>
> "What you should say"—he told me—"what you should
> say is that you want to be a saint."
>
> A saint! The thought struck me as a little weird. I said,
> "How do you expect me to become a saint?"
>
> "By wanting to," said Lax, simply . . . "Don't you believe
> that God will make you what He created you to be, if you
> will consent to let Him do it?"[16]

Remember the "whisky priest" and his final realization?
"(T)hat it would have been quite easy to have been a saint." (*TPTG,*
251) *Is it really?* Then what would that sanctity look like?

16. Thomas Merton, *The Seven Storey Mountain*, 233-34.

10. The Sanctuary of Saints in Richard Rodriguez's "Late Victorians"

Days of Obligation

In Richard Rodriguez's memoir, *Days of Obligation, An Argument with My Mexican Father,* the author writes about sanctity in the chapter entitled "Late Victorians." It begins, fittingly I would say, with St. Augustine's insight that something is wrong:

> St. Augustine writes from his cope of dust that we are restless hearts, for earth is not our true home. Human unhappiness is evidence of our immortality. Intuition tells us we are meant for some other city. ("LV," *DO,* 26)

Rodriguez is an American of Mexican descent; born in San Francisco, raised in Sacramento, schooled by Irish nuns at Sacred Heart Church and keenly adept at the sacramental way of seeing. He is also a gay man, living alone in a San Francisco apartment that has been chopped from a whole nineteenth century Victorian home. Rodriguez is a journalist, a teacher, and a practicing Catholic. The "Late Victorian" is the house. The place is San Francisco at a time when the AIDS epidemic of the 1980s ravaged its population like nobody's business.

> *"And the saints of this city*
> *have names listed in the phone book . . ."*

In a manner that is similar to Annie Dillard's *Holy the Firm*, Rodriguez gives us stacks of images depicting his particular world as a single man living in a house that was built, three stories high, for three generations of family. Now there are "four single men . . . living against the expectations of nature." All around him are examples of the façade of their existence: the veneer of beauty, the fakery of painted stone, the prettifying of a culture and an architecture not built for them.

> The nineteenth-century mirror over the fireplace in my bedroom was purchased by a decorator from the estate of a man who died last year of AIDS. It is a top-heavy piece, confusing styles. Two ebony-painted columns support a frieze of painted glass above the free-range cherubs. The lake of the mirror has formed a cataract, and at its edges it is beginning to corrode. . . . ("LV," *DO,* 40)

He speaks of the memory of mirrors which held images that have long since passed away; memories "not mine." He speaks of the optimism of gay young men who arrived in San Francisco looking for a utopia, and found tragedy. "If I respond to the metaphor of spring, I nevertheless learned, years ago, from my Mexican father, from my Irish nuns, to count on winter." ("LV," *DO,* 29) He speaks of his own skepticism and of the futility of those trying to adorn a world too well dotted with sin.

> I found the company of men who pursued an earthly paradise charming. Skepticism became my demeanor toward them—I was the dinner-party skeptic, a firm believer in Original Sin and in the limits of possibility. Which charmed them. ("LV," *DO,* 41-42)

And he speaks of death. "Into this world falls . . . " (not a plane).

> Four years ago on a Sunday in winter—a brilliant spring afternoon—I was jogging near Fort Point while overhead a young woman was, with difficulty, climbing over the railing of the Golden Gate Bridge. Holding down her skirt with one hand, with the other she waved to a startled spectator . . . before she stepped onto the sky. To land like a spilled purse at my feet. ("LV," *DO,* 27)

We are no strangers to tragedy. We all make pretty our worlds, our interior spaces, our yards, our bodies, our children. But life has a way of catching us up to calamity. Parents die, then friends, siblings, spouses, maybe children, and on it goes. Here the young die by the thousands, consumed by this dreaded disease of the blood. But these deaths are not like the charming deaths one reads about in Victorian novels, with custard puddings, drawn curtains, straw-strewn streets. AIDS would ravage the populace, and it would not be tidy. Rodriguez warns us that there is no way to pretty-up a death from AIDS. His friend, César, he tells us, "experienced agony."

> The phone rang. AIDS had tagged a friend. And then the phone rang again. And then the phone rang again. ("LV," *DO,* 42)

People came, to visit, to help where they could; family, when there was family.

> Sometimes no family came. If there was family, it was usually Mother. Mom. With her suitcase and with the torn flap of an envelope in her hand. . . . Or parents came but then left without reconciliation, some preferring to say 'cancer.'
>
> But others came. They walked Death's dog. They washed his dishes. They bought his groceries. They massaged his poor back. . . . Men who sought the aesthetic order of existence were recalled to nature. . . . And if gays took care of their own, they were not alone. AIDS was a disease of the entire city. . . . Others came. There were nurses and nuns and the couple from next door, co-workers, strangers. . . . A community was forming over the city. ("LV," *DO,* 45)

In his essay, Rodriguez takes into account that which is ordinary in our lives (a house, a mirror, a city, a jog in the park) as having extraordinary significance; and then those things that ought to be most extraordinary (death and human compassion) as quite routine. This juxtaposing angle, this new way of seeing, should be familiar territory to us by now. It is sacramental language, taking what is commonplace (a bridge, a car, a tattoo, a moth, a hog) and seeing it as something so significant that it is in contact with mystery and the underlying presence of God. In touch with, in touch with, in touch with.

Recall Wendy M. Wright's take on the Catholic imagination: "We are bound to see the finite world as the bearer of the infinite and we must consider that which is singular as of nearly infinite significance. The finite and the infinite are inseparably bound. We find God in the ironic juxtaposition of our most fervent hopes and our experience of the sorrow of the world."[1]

Recall Annie Dillard's cruciform in *Holy the Firm*.

In "Late Victorians," sorrow abounds. It is not the sorrow we find in novels, Victorian or otherwise. It is not like literature. Sorrow, when in the concrete, enfleshed, suffering people that live and breathe around us—even a hand's reach away—is more real than any story. Sorrow moves us to see the other as an other Christ. Sorrow is the gift of God. We who love literature can miss this crucial point, because we do need to pull our heads out of the pages and look around; visit a nursing home, sweep a floor, serve a meal, go to Mount Everest.

There is sorrow, yes, and great suffering, but there are heroes, too. We find them in unexpected places.

> And the saints of this city have names listed in the phone book, names I heard called through a microphone one cold Sunday in Advent as I sat in Most Holy Redeemer Church. . . . A woman at the microphone called upon volunteers from the AIDS Support Group to come forward. Throughout the church, people stood up . . . shy at being called. Yet they came forward and assembled in the sanctuary, facing the congregation, grinning self-consciously at one another, their hands hidden behind them.
>
> I am preoccupied by the fussing of a man sitting in the pew directly in front of me—in his seventies, frail, his iodine-colored hair combed forward and pasted upon his forehead. . . . And then he rises, this old monkey, with

1. Wright, "Jesuit Schloesser Weaves Tapestry of Catholic Imagination."

the most beatific dignity, in answer to the microphone, and he strides into the sanctuary to take his place in the company of the Blessed.

So this is it—this, what looks like a Christmas party in an insurance office, and not as in Renaissance paintings, and not as we had always thought. . . . A lady with a plastic candy cane pinned to her lapel. A Castro clone with a red bandana exploding from his hip pocket. A perfume counter lady with an Hermès scarf mantled upon her shoulder. A black man in a checkered sports coat. The pink-haired punkess with a jewel in her nose. Here, too, is the gay couple in middle age; interchangeable plaid shirts and corduroy pants. . . . These know the weight of bodies. . . . These learned to love what is corruptible, while I, barren skeptic, reader of St. Augustine, curator of the earthly paradise, inheritor of the empty mirror, I shift my tailbone upon the cold, hard pew. ("LV," *DO*, 45-47.)

What is it that "looks like a Christmas party" and "not as in Renaissance paintings?" The communion of saints! What is more ordinary than an office party speckled with odd, self-conscious, shy people? What is more significant than the communion of saints? Rodriguez gets it! The Word was made flesh and became *man*. God humbled Himself to share in our awkward humanity. Our words (of preaching, teaching, singing, praying) are made flesh by our *actions* done in love. To know the weight of bodies, dignified and sanctified bodies (made so by Christ Incarnate), bodies that fall (off of bridges, off the wagon, out of grace or the natural order), is to know the mercy of Christ. And to share in serving the poor and sick among us, by cooking a meal, or walking a dog, or sweeping a floor, or wiping a bottom, this is to share in Christ's inexhaustible love.

Why is there such suffering? Who can say? Not Merton, not Dillard, not Rodriguez, not we, but there is something to do about it; because here we are—we who call ourselves Christians—shifting our tired tailbones and crying like babies.

11. The Sacrament of Sacraments

Conclusion

IT IS MY HOPE that this journey has allowed an inward pause and directional shift that points the reader outward towards the world. As we speak the name we were given at our baptism and discern what is expected of us, we should stop to recognize the guides we have met along the way; saints, poets, and all.

Well, what is expected of us? We fall, we sin, we ask forgiveness; we suffer a worldly existence but we are not of the world. We do not etch our sins into our flesh as some hideous, human judgment (Kafka); or discount the burnt bodies of children (Dillard); or shun the bodies corrupted by AIDS (Rodriguez). No. We were born to have a body (Camus). We put on God. We tattoo Christ in our flesh (O'Connor). We light the string of our gut (Dillard). We climb onto the cross with compassion, not to be better seen by others (Camus), but to share in the passion of Christ as an act of sacrificial love (Merton). Our authors knew this: to learn how to see (Dillard) in order to recognize the suffering of others; to see the truth of our given reality (O'Connor), a reality that is charged with the grandeur of God (Hopkins); to be the nun for the burnt girl (Dillard); to sleep on the ground for a friend (Camus); to stand with the saints in Holy Redeemer Church (Rodriguez); to know the weight of bodies and love what is corruptible (Rodriguez); to fulfill our life's calling (Greene); to love other people (Merton); to go at our lives with a broadax (Dillard); to be Christ for the world (Merton).

Jesus told us he would not leave us orphaned. He sent us the Holy Spirit and gave us the church, the sacraments, the gospels. He revealed to us as a sacramental sign the revelation that God is a relationship of love. These gifts require a response. What is your unique path in the passion of Christ? What is your passion? What is the love and the center of your existence?

The Center of Existence

In a letter to a friend, Flannery O'Connor described her relationship with the love of her life. One evening she was taken to a dinner party with some intellectual, literary friends and found herself feeling quite out of place in such company.

> Having me there was like having a dog present who had been trained to say a few words but, overcome with inadequacy, had forgotten them. Well, toward morning the conversation turned on the Eucharist, which I, being the Catholic, was obviously supposed to defend. [Our hostess said that she] thought of it as a symbol and implied that it was a pretty good one. I then said, in a very shaky voice, "Well, if it's a symbol, to hell with it." That was all the defense I was capable of, but I realize now that this is all I will ever be able to say about it, outside of a story, except that it is the center of existence for me; all the rest of life is expendable.[1]

"The center of existence." Didn't you know? When we participate in the Eucharist we *are* Eucharist, we *are* communion, we are the body of Christ that is the church. And this church, this people, this tattered remnant of Eden, is flawed, varied, broken, often sinful, yet always and profoundly *sacramental*. Our words and actions in the world, our "outward sign of an invisible grace," are critical to our character, because we embody Christ to those we encounter. That is our Christian vocation. We are called to "reproduce in our own lives the life and sufferings and charity

---

1. Fitzgerald, *Flannery O'Connor, The Habit of Being,* 125.

of Christ in a way unknown to anyone else who has ever lived under the sun."[2]

As the living body of Christ, we are an enduring church that *breathes*, and our breath is stories. Didn't you know? Didn't you take up Jean-Baptiste's mirror and look? *We are those stories!*

Ah-ha! The trick is played! Not Jean-Baptiste's sly swindle—that crafty judge-penitent who was quick to show his fellows their sinful selves but then cower under the blankets lest grace catch hold. Yes, it begins with sin but it does not end there. Take a look in this new mirror and never forget that you were purchased at a great price; you were redeemed by God's own Sacrament. You bear the infinite God in your very flesh. This is not mere metaphor but our deepest reality. God is visible to the world because *you* are sacramental! *You* are that sign!

So be of good cheer, "When the Word became Flesh, it assumed the universe."[3]

Then an angel took it in his hand and brought it to me and said,
'This must thou eat,' and I ate the world [4]

2. Merton, *No Man is an Island*, 95.

3. Fowlie, "Catholic Orientation in Contemporary French Literature," 241.

4. Ralph Waldo Emerson, as quoted by Annie Dillard in *Pilgrim at Tinker Creek*, 271.

Review Questions

THE FOLLOWING REVIEW QUESTIONS are provided for your use in the classroom or in a book club setting. They are also provided to encourage your further study of the material.

Chapter 1: The Sacramental Imagination

- What do you think about salvation taking place, instrumentally, through the human body?
- Can you think of examples of bodily worship?
- How do Catholic themes differ from Protestant themes, in literature and in theology?
- If you are or were a Protestant, what do you think about these differences? Are they expressions of your own experiences?
- Can you identify key works that express the Protestant imagination?
- What makes a story uniquely "Catholic?" Is it the author's faith; the author's sensibilities; stories of saints, priests or nuns; Bing Crosby?
- How might these qualities influence future writers who are Catholic?

Chapter 2: Stories and Sacraments

- What is your earliest memory? Is it of a thing outside your own thoughts? Is there an emotion attached? A person? A story?

- How would you embellish that story?

- What are the aspects and structures of a story?

- What is a literary symbol?

- What are the seven sacraments?

- What is the matter and form of any particular sacrament?

- What is the first sacrament?

- What are the matter and form of baptism?

- What is its purpose?

- Are the sacraments symbols?

- How is a sacrament different from a literary symbol? An allegory? A metaphor?

Chapter 3: Original Sin and Baptism in Albert Camus' *The Fall*

- What does the doctrine of original sin tell us?

- Is the world as it ought to be?

- What is the protagonist's name in *The Fall*? Is it his real name?

- What is he like?

- What is his world like? Where is it? Can you describe it?

- What is he in exile from?

- What is he choosing to forget?

- Yet the work is a recollection. Why a recollection?

- What is he guilty of?

- Does he recognize his guilt?
- What does his humiliating experience teach him, when he is smacked in the head at the intersection?
- What is a judge-penitent? Why a judge? Why a penitent?
- What is the significance of the doves?
- Do the doves ever descend? When? Do you know why? What will they bring?
- What is Jean-Baptiste's response to the doves?
- Why doesn't he go outside?
- What is grace? Does Jean-Baptiste believe in grace?
- Do you see yourself in Jean-Baptiste's mirror?
- Does *The Fall* strike you as a religious book?

Chapter 4: Guilt and Penance in Flannery O'Connor's *Wise Blood*

- What is guilt? How is guilt usually portrayed in our culture? In our faith tradition?
- What is the world of Taulkinham like?
- Why is this world so dark?
- What is the protagonist, Hazel Motes, like?
- Who / what is Enoch Emery? In what way might he be compared to Jonah? What is his wise blood?
- Discuss the relationship between Asa Hawks and his daughter, Sabbath Lilly.
- How does sight play into the story?
- What is Hazel running from?
- What is his burden? What are his sins? What else?
- What significance does the Essex (car) have in the story?
- What is the "new jesus" like? How is he imaged for us?

- Why do you think this "new jesus" is portrayed as a dried-up mummy?
- How does Solace Layfield play into the story? What might his name signify?
- Who does he resemble? Why might that be important?
- What becomes of Enoch Emery?
- How are the themes of *The Fall* and *Wise Blood* similar?
- Where does God reveal Himself in *Wise Blood*?
- How is Hazel's response to humiliation different from Jean-Baptiste's?
- Why does Hazel respond with mortification?
- What do you think Mrs. Flood will do with Hazel's dead body?
- Is there any hope for her? How do you know that?

Chapter 5: The Dilemma of Sight in Annie Dillard's *Pilgrim at Tinker Creek*

- With regard to original sin and the fall of mankind, what does Annie Dillard seem to be saying in the frog and giant bug scene?
- What is Dillard's dilemma? Would you take sides: either the earth my mother is a monster, or I am a freak?
- Why do animals suffer? Did nature fall when Adam and Eve were banished from paradise?
- Is there evil in nature? Suffering? Loss? Grief?
- Will your beloved pets go to heaven?
- Do you think all of nature will return to God in a reunification or restoration of all of creation?
- Who is Origen of Alexandria, do you know?

- Does this view of Origen mesh with current Catholic thought, influenced by St. Thomas?

- Origen's ideas splinter off of the branch of Christian Catholicism as we know it today, yet his questions linger as a problem. They also exist in other aspects of Christian thought which emphasize the distance of God from Creation. Can you identify them?

Chapter 6: The Poetry of Incarnation

- Gerard Manley Hopkins was a convert, a Jesuit priest and a poet. In "God's Grandeur" the world is charged with God (not removed from God). How does the poem present this idea?

- What images does Hopkins use?

- Why is creation, in this telling, bursting with God-imagery? What happened?

- Human toil is exhausting, but there exists in nature an underlying sweetness. Because?

- Describe the falcon in "The Windhover."

- To whom does Hopkins compare the bird? What other images apply?

- The cut earth shines from the sharp blade of a plow; and embers, though bleak and black, gash glory when they break open. Compare these images to Jesus Christ, crucified.

- Is the world fallen, or is it a mirror of the beauty of God?

- Who is Hagia Sophia? What does the name mean? Is she a person, a metaphor, an aspect of God?

- How many analogies can you find with regard to Sophia? She is like . . . . she is like . . . .

- What does she give to God?

- What does she give to the world?

- What is the Incarnation?

- What is the legacy of the Incarnation? Can you identify the many gifts that Christ's entry into human history affords us?

- How are other people portrayed in Thomas Merton's journal post, at Fourth and Walnut?

- Contrast his view with the view of Hazel Motes or Enoch Emery in Taulkinham. What happened? Why is Merton's way of seeing so different?

- What is the legacy of the Incarnation? Can you list them? List everything you can think of, in gratitude.

Chapter 7: The Incarnation and Grace in Flannery O'Connor's "Parker's Back" and "Revelation"

- Without the sanctification of human life, we are left to human judgment and human punishment. This notion is depicted in Kafka's "In the Penal Colony," explain how.

- What is inscribed in the condemned man's flesh?

- What is the point of giving the tortured man warm rice pudding?

- Can atheists be moral? Upon what will they base their morality? Kafka was a non-practicing Jew. Upon what do the Jewish people base their morality? And Christians?

- What might Pope Benedict XVI mean by the "tyranny of the majority" in his condemnation of moral relativism?

- What justifies punishment? What is its purpose?

- When is the action of grace offered, if it is offered, in Kafka's story? Why do you think that is?

- When the human body is desecrated, how does that reflect upon our human dignity? The Incarnation?

- Can you give other examples of bodily sacrilege present in our society?

- Explain why Flannery O'Connor chose a tattoo to illustrate her story, "Parker's Back."

- Describe Sarah-Ruth. What does she look like?

- Why is Sara-Ruth such a bad cook? Why is she against color?

- What is Sarah-Ruth's heresy?

- What is Docetism?

- Describe O. E. Parker. What inspired him most as a child?

- Why does he marry Sarah-Ruth?

- What happens to O. E. Parker that knocks him off his horse, so to speak? Does this remind you of any biblical persons?

- How does Parker respond?

- Why did he choose a tattoo of Jesus Christ? How does this change him?

- How does he gain entry into his house?

- Why does Sarah-Ruth react with violence and beat the tattooed image of Christ?

- Why does Parker cry like a baby?

- What do we mean by "the action of grace" in a story? In a Catholic story?

- What is grace, in the Catholic sense of the word?

- Describe Ruby Turpin.

- How is she like Jean-Baptiste? Could she be described as a judge-penitent?

- What biblical stories does "Revelation" recall? What biblical characters?

- Can you find three moments in the story where grace is offered?

- What does the title of the short story reveal to you? What is the revelation?

- Has Ruby Turpin been prepared to receive it? How?
- What is the name of the ugly college girl?
- Regarding the vision of the heavenly procession at the end of the story, why are the sensible folk ascending with shocked faces, as even their virtues are purged away? Why their virtues?
- How is Ruby Turpin unlike Jean-Baptiste?
- What is the cost of redemption?

Chapter 8: The Vocation of Love in Graham Greene's *The Power and the Glory*

- In the Catholic Church, what are the two sacraments of vocation?
- What is the function of the priest in the world?
- What is unique or particular about the vocation of the priest?
- What is the name of the "whisky priest?"
- What is his world like?
- How is the "whisky priest" like Hazel Motes? Like Ruby Turpin?
- How is the priesthood depicted in *The Power and the Glory*?
- Is there a particularly powerful action in the story that can be described as an "action of grace," which changes the characters?
- Who is the half-caste? How does he play a role in the priest's salvation?
- Does the unbelieving Lieutenant play a similar role? How or how not?
- Who are the Lehrs, and why do you suppose Greene included this odd side-step in his story?

- How is the priest saved?
- Where is the glory of his martyrdom?
- Why can't he stand up when he is brought to the place of execution?
- How is the glory of his martyrdom finally revealed to us in this book?
- What does the mother now say about him to her children?
- Is the "whisky priest" a saint? Why, or why not?
- Is there any significance, at the end of the book, that the new priest does not finish telling the boy his name? What is the significance?
- What is your name in baptism? Can you speak it? Will you?
- What is the price of redemption?

Chapter 9: The Point of Suffering in Annie Dillard's *Holy the Firm*

- What does it mean to not only accept suffering but to make it holy? How does one make suffering holy?
- How did Jesus die?
- Which characters in the studied works best personify this tremendous love?
- What does it mean when St. Paul says that we are baptized into the death of Christ?
- How did Job's friends sin?
- In *Holy the Firm*, Annie Dillard says that "All day long I feel created." What might she mean by this?
- How does she make the reader experience this 'created' feeling that she experiences?
- In *Pilgrim at Tinker Creek*, Dillard emphasized the importance of seeing. In *Wise Blood*, O'Connor does the same.

Even in *The Fall*, the protagonist helps and then degrades the blind. Why is sight so important in these stories? (It doesn't have to be sight, it could be sound, or touch, or taste, but for these works, it is sight).

- What happened to Julie Norwich?
- How does one make the suffering of children holy? Can it be done, should it?
- Can you name at least five examples of repeating images that you come across in *Holy the Firm*. Are they linked, somehow, in kind with one another? Can you link them?
- What two paths does Dillard describe in the closing pages of the book? Can you trace them in history? What great thinkers might be set upon each path? Do they ever come together?
- What is the point of *Holy the Firm*?
- What is Dillard's resolution at the end of the book? Is it enough?

Chapter 10: The Sanctuary of Saints in Richard Rodriguez's "Late Victorians"

- What does St. Augustine mean when he says that human unhappiness is evidence of our immortality? What other place are we meant for?
- How many examples of human unhappiness and tragedy can you find in this essay?
- Discuss Rodriguez's juxtaposing of public and private lives.
- How many examples of faux nature can you find?
- What would a Christian realist like O'Connor, for example, have to say about the painted rockery, the empty mirror, the Victorian house housing four bachelors?
- Why is the language of this essay so graphic and disturbing?

- St. Thomas says that grace does not destroy nature, but perfects it. How might this notion be applied to Rodriguez's essay?

- Why are the volunteers at Holy Redeemer Church called by name to the sanctuary? Can you describe them? What would a Renaissance painting and a Christmas office party have in common?

- When the old man, "this old monkey," rises to his name, he does so with "beatific dignity." What might this imply? Do you share it?

Appendix 1

First Thought—1958

It was, I can suppose now, an ordinary day, but it was not ordinary to me—except perhaps in the sacred sense of a day well-ordered in time. But that is in retrospect. What I remember then is an angled room divided by bars. And over the bars, through a bright white square, a pleasing block of peach burned brilliant on a field of pastel rose. There was no blue. There never was. There was only this long, amber wedge which, when watched, narrowed ever so slowly—as if it had all the time in the world, as if it had a whole long lifetime ahead.

How could I know that this was just a shaft of light from the setting sun, striking the ordinary pink stucco of a ticky-tacky wall on the too-close house next door? How could I comprehend the slow rotation of the earth, circling a nuclear star whose photons danced upon the rosy retina of my fresh new eyes? How could I care? I was too much in love with the sudden and charming notion that I, somehow, was I.

Bibliography

New American Bible. Iowa Falls, Iowa: World Bible Publications, 1987.

Douay-Rheims Catholic Bible. New York: Douay Bible House, 1941.

Barron, Bishop Robert. "Creation and Beauty." *Christian Life Community,* Gonzaga University. http://www.gonzaga.edu/About/Mission/University-Ministry/programs/CLC-Meeting-Resources.asp.

Camus, Albert. *The Fall.* Translated by Justin O'Brien, 1956. New York: Vintage, Alfred A. Knopf. Originally published in France as *La Chute.* Librairie Gallimard, 1956.

————. "An Absurd Reasoning." In *The Myth of Sisyphus and Other Essays.* Translated by Justin O'Brien, 3-48. New York: Vintage, Alfred A. Knopf, 1955. Originally published in France as *Le Mythe de Sisyphe,* Librairie Gallimard, 1942.

————. "The Unbeliever and Christians." In *Resistance, Rebellion, and Death.* Translated by Justin O'Brien, 69-74. New York: Alfred A. Knopf, 1961. Essays originally published in France by Librairie Gallimard, 1958.

Caranfa, Angelo. *Claudel, Beauty and Grace.* Cranbury, New Jersey: Associated University Presses, 1989.

Chesterton, G. K. *Orthodoxy.* New York: Image, Doubleday, 1959. Dodd, Mead and Co., 1908.

Clark, Mary T., ed. *An Aquinas Reader, Selections from the Writings of Thomas Aquinas.* New York: Image; Doubleday, 1972.

Doran, Robert M., and John D. Dadosky, eds. *Collected Works of Bernard Lonergan: Method in Theology,* 56. Toronto: University of Toronto Press, 1972.

Dillard, Annie. *Holy the Firm.* New York: Harper and Row, Colophon, 1977.

————. *Pilgrim at Tinker Creek.* New York: Harper and Row, 1974.

Eliot, T. S. "Poetry and Propaganda." The Bookman. February (1930) http://www.unz.org/Pub/Bookman-1930feb-00595

Fowlie, Wallace. "Catholic Orientation in Contemporary French Literature." In *Spiritual Problems in Contemporary Literature,* edited by Stanley Romaine Hopper, 225-241. New York: Harper and Row, 1952.

Garvey, John. "Something is Wrong: That's the Beginning of Wisdom." *Commonweal,* 141 (2014) 8.

Giannone, Richard. *Flannery O'Connor and the Mystery of Love.* Chicago: University of Illinois Press, 1989.

Greeley, Andrew. *The Catholic Imagination.* University of California Press, 2000.

———. *The Catholic Myth: The Behavior and Beliefs of American Catholics.* New York: Macmillan, 1990.

———. "Why I'm Still A Catholic." http://www.agreeley.com/articles/why. html.

Greene, Graham. *The Power and the Glory.* New York: Viking, 1940. Reprint Time, Inc., 1962.

———. *A Sort of Life.* New York: Simon and Schuster, 1971.

Heartney, Eleanor. "Blood, Sex, and Blasphemy-The Catholic Imagination in Contemporary Art." New Art Examiner, 26.6 March (1999) 1-8.

Holy See, *Catechism of the Catholic Church.* New York: Image, Doubleday, 1995. Libreria Editrice Vaticana, Latin Text, 1994.

Hopkins, Gerard Manley. *Poems of Gerard Manley Hopkins.* Edited by Robert Bridges. London: Humphrey Milford, XCVIII.

Kafka, Franz. "In the Penal Colony." In *The Penal Colony: Stories and Short Pieces,*191-227. New York: Schocken Books, 1948.

Mabry, Donald J. "Mexican Anticlerics, Bishops, Cristeros, and the Devout during the 1920s: A Scholarly Debate," *Journal of Church and State,* Vol. 20, No. 1 (1978) 81-92.

Merton, Thomas. *Conjectures of a Guilty Bystander.* New York: Doubleday, 1966.

———. "Hagia Sophia." In *Emblems of a Season of Fury,* 61-69. New York: New Directions, 1961.

———. *No Man is an Island.* New York: Dell, 1955.

———. *The Seven Storey Mountain.* New York: Harcourt, Brace, 1948.

———. *A Thomas Merton Reader,* edited by Thomas P. McDonnell. New York: Image, Doubleday, 1974.

Milton, John. *Paradise Lost and Selected Poetry and Prose.* Holt, Rinehart and Winston, 1964.

Mumma, Howard. *Albert Camus and the Minister.* Brewster, Massachusetts: Paraclete, 2000.

O'Connor, Flannery. *Collected Works.* New York: Library of America, 1988.

———. *The Habit of Being: Letters of Flannery O'Connor, Selected and Edited by Sally Fitzgerald.* New York: Farrar, Straus and Giroux, 1979.

———. *Mystery and Manners, Occasional Prose, selected and edited by Sally and Robert Fitzgerald.* New York: Farrar, Straus and Giroux, 1957.

Pearce, Joseph. "Graham Greene, Doubter Par Excellence." Catholic Education Resource Center (2001), http://www.catholiceducation.org/en/culture/art/ graham-greene-doubter-par-excellence.html.

Pramuk, Christopher. *Sophia, The Hidden Christ of Thomas Merton.* Collegeville, Minnesota: Liturgical Press, 2009.

Radcliffe, Timothy, OP. *What is the Point of Being a Christian?* New York: Burns and Oats, Continuum, 2005.

Rodriguez, Richard. *Days of Obligation: An Argument with My Mexican Father.* New York: Penguin, 1992.

Safina, Carl. *Beyond Words: What Animals Think and Feel.* New York: Henry Holt, 2015.

Schillebeeckx, Edward, OP. *Christ the Sacrament of Encounter with God.* New York: Sheed and Ward, 1963.

Shawn, Wallace and Gregory, André. *My Dinner With André, A Screenplay for the Film by Louis Malle.* New York: Grove, 1981.

Toolan, David S., SJ. "At Home in the Cosmos: The Poetics of Matter=Energy" *America*, 174.6 (1996) 8–14.

Turnell, Martin. *Baudelaire, A Study of his Poetry.* NY: New Directions, 1972.

Van Hove, Brian, SJ. Review of "Blood-Drenched Altars" by Francis Clement Kelly. "Baltimore's Archbishop Michael Joseph Curley, Oklahoma's Bishop Francis Clement Kelley and the Mexican Affair: 1934-1936." 1-10. http://www.ewtn.com/library/homelibr/fr94204.txt. [References *The Baltimore Catholic Review,* April 19 and August 23, 1935.]

Wright, Wendy M. "Jesuit Schloesser Weaves Tapestry of Catholic Imagination." *Journal of Religion & Society* 9 (1998) http://www.moses.creighton.edu/csrs/news/S98-3.html.

Made in the USA
Coppell, TX
21 December 2020

46888174R00085